The Redemption of the King

LeBron James
Returns to Cleveland!

Vince McKee

CLERISY PRESS

The Redemption of the King: LeBron James Returns to Cleveland!

For further information, please contact the publisher:

CLERISY PRESS
An imprint of Keen Communications, LLC
306 Greenup St.
Covington, KY 41011
clerisypress.com

Library of Congress Cataloging-in-Publication Data

McKee, Vince.
    The redemption of the King : LeBron James returns to Cleveland / by Vince McKee.
      pages cm
    Summary: "LeBron James is back in Cleveland's court, and the city is on fire as its chosen one has decided to come home. His highly publicized, and equally highly emotional, return to Cleveland reveals his penultimate goal: to bring a championship back to northeast Ohio where he grew up. Now, for the first time ever, the full story is told from the beginning as author Vince McKee covers James's entire journey in every detail both on and off the court—from the start of his career with the Cavaliers in Cleveland to his departure to Miami, his time with the Heat, and finally, the much debated and highly anticipated return of the "King." Although pro basketball is an international juggernaut in terms of dollars, this story revolves more around hometown pride and character than money or celebrity." — Provided by publisher.
    ISBN 978-1-57860-571-2 (paperback) — ISBN 1-57860-571-7 () — eISBN 0 978-1-57860-572-9
    1. James, LeBron. 2. Basketball players—United States—Biography. 3. Cleveland Cavaliers (Basketball team) 4. Basketball—Ohio—Cleveland. I. Title.
    GV884.J36M45 2015
    796.323092—dc23
    [B]

2014047451

Distributed by Publishers Group West
Printed in the United States of America
First edition, first printing

Editor: Vanessa Lynn Rusch
Cover design: Scott McGrew
Text design: Annie Long
Front-cover photo: © Keith Allison / Wikimedia Commons / CC-BY-SA 3.0
Back-cover photo: © Vince McKee
Copyeditor: Emily C. Beaumont
Indexer: Rich Carlson

This book is dedicated to my brother, Don, and his wife, Abbie.

You have both always been my number-one fans

and a major reason I never gave up. I love you both!

This book is also dedicated to Braylon and Bret—

May your souls forever rest in peace,

as heaven has its two newest and most beautiful angels.

Contents

Acknowledgments

I want to thank first my incredible wife, Emily, and our adorable daughter, Maggie, for giving me the time and space to do this project on such a short notice, after I had planned on taking some time off. I would like to thank the hardworking and loyal fans of Cleveland, who never gave up hope. I would also like to thank my parents, Don and Maria McKee, for a lifetime of support; my wife's parents, Bob and Deborah Lamb, for always believing in me and making me feel so welcome in their family; Kenny Roda, Ken Carman, and Jerry Mires for dropping everything at a moment's notice for some quick interviews; and Jim Friguglietti for his continued guidance. Most importantly, I want to thank my Lord and Savior, Jesus Christ, as it is through His light that all work is done.

The Cavaliers became an NBA franchise in 1970 under owner Nick Mileti.

Photo: Sam Bourquin

Introduction

LeBron James is regarded by many as the greatest player in the history of high school basketball and is seen as having the potential to surpass Michael Jordan as the game's greatest player of all time. In the early 2000s, because of his incoming talent, most NBA experts considered LeBron to be better than 75 percent of the then-current league's talent before he played even one game. So it was no surprise when he forfeited his college eligibility and declared he would enter the 2003 NBA draft. For the Cavaliers, the chance to select LeBron as their first overall pick signaled a rebirth for the franchise, as well as for the city of Cleveland.

On May 22, 2003, after five years of no luck, Cleveland finally turned around their fate when they won the NBA draft lottery. The reason why the number-one pick was so crucial was that LeBron would be entering the draft. The Cavaliers were tied with the Denver Nuggets for the highest chance of winning the pick. It almost seemed like a dream come true for Cleveland fans, who, for so many years prior, had received every bad bounce of the ball and wrong turn along the way. Most fans stopped believing that good things could actually happen for their beloved teams. The fans had survived a drive, a fumble, a shot, Jose Mesa, and even their beloved Cleveland Browns leaving town, and now, for the first time in many years, something had finally gone their way. Legendary Cavaliers alumni Austin Carr was so moved with emotion by the lottery results that he was seen in tears following the announcement. Never before had the bounce of a little white lottery ball carried so much weight for the hopes and dreams of so many fans. The winds of change were finally blowing on the cold shores of Northeast Ohio, and its war-torn fans were set to receive some long-awaited hope at last.

On paper, LeBron had every right to leave Cleveland as a free agent when his contract expired in the summer of 2010, which simply stated that he was drafted by the Cavaliers—not that he had chosen to play there. On paper, LeBron didn't owe Cleveland anything more than his best effort, which he gave in full. However, life is based on so much more than what is written down on paper.

CHAPTER ONE

The Chosen One

LeBron James was born on December 30, 1984. He shares a birthday with other great athletes, such as Tiger Woods and Sandy Koufax. Perhaps this was an early sign that the young man was destined for greatness.

His mother, Gloria Marie James, was 16 years old when LeBron was born, and she raised the young prodigy on her own in Akron, Ohio. In an attempt to find stable work and a brighter future for her son, Gloria allowed LeBron to move in with the family of Frank Walker, a local youth football coach, who introduced LeBron to basketball when he was 9 years old. LeBron was instantly a star on the court, as he excelled playing with the Northeast Ohio Shooting Stars in the Amateur Athletic Union, more commonly known as AAU basketball. The team, led by LeBron and his friends, enjoyed success on first a regional and then on a national level.

LeBron chose to attend St. Vincent–St. Mary High School, which was well known for its athletics and high academic standards. He was a star athlete from the first moment his feet touched the gym floor at St. Vincent–St. Mary. In his freshman year, LeBron averaged 21 points and 6 rebounds per game for the school's varsity team. He led St. Vincent–St. Mary to a perfect 27–0 record and a Division III State Title championship win. In his sophomore year, LeBron averaged 25.2 points and 7.2 rebounds, 5.8 assists, and 3.8 steals per game. A number of the team's home games had to be relocated to the University of Akron as the demand was so high to see LeBron play, and the 5,492-seat Rhodes Arena would sell out in minutes of tickets going on sale. NBA players who were in town to face the Cavaliers, including Michael Jordan, would drive out to Akron just to see him play. The hype around LeBron grew by the moment, and at the young age of 16, he was slated to be the next big thing in sports. There was demand from alumni, local fans, and college and NBA scouts who all wanted to see LeBron play.

His sophomore year was every bit as successful as his freshman year, and the team went 26–1 for the season and again won the state championship. LeBron was named Ohio's Mr. Basketball and was selected to play with the *USA Today* All-USA High School Basketball First Team—the first-ever high school sophomore to do either. As LeBron's success on the court spread, so did media interest in his talent. Prior to the beginning of his junior year at St. Vincent–St. Mary, LeBron appeared in *SLAM* magazine, touted as potentially "the best high school basketball player in America right now," according to Ryan Jones, former editor-in-chief of the publication. Later on in the season, LeBron would go on to be featured on the cover of *Sports Illustrated* magazine—the first underclassman high school basketball player to do so.

LeBron continued his dominance as a junior by averaging 29 points, 8.3 rebounds, 5.7 assists, and 3.3 steals per game. It was no surprise when he was once again named Ohio's Mr. Basketball and selected to the *USA Today* All-USA High School Basketball First Team. LeBron quieted any remaining media analysts that had doubts about his talent when he also became the first junior to win the

Gatorade National Player of the Year Award. St. Vincent–St. Mary would go on to end the season at 23–4 with a loss at the Division II championship game.

LeBron took his show on the road his senior year, as the St. Vincent–St. Mary Fighting Irish traveled around the country to play a number of nationally ranked teams, including a game against Oak Hill Academy that was nationally televised on ESPN2. Additionally, Time Warner Cable even offered a cable pay-per-view package for dedicated fans to order just to watch him play. LeBron would go on to give pay-per-view buyers their money's worth, as he averaged 31.6 points, 9.6 rebounds, 4.6 assists, and 3.4 steals per game. Once again, for an unprecedented third consecutive year, LeBron was named Ohio's Mr. Basketball and selected for the *USA Today* All-USA First Team, and he was named as the Gatorade National Player of the Year for the second year in a row. The remarkable year concluded with another state championship win for the Fighting Irish.

Those in the local media believed that LeBron would soon become the next big thing in the NBA. Ken Carman, night host for Cleveland's 92.3 The Fan sports radio, shared his insights on LeBron and his immediate impact on the league:

I think because of him, he made mild basketball fans rabid basketball fans because he was just so great. I was still in high school when he debuted, and I even knew he would make a team look so much better, despite how much we all expected that first season. He was doing some remarkable things, and I felt that all the hype over him was real. I knew there would be some growing pains, such as the trouble he had with an actual jump shot and some defensive issues. It's amazing because we sit there and preach defense all day long because we watch teams like San Antonio, and we use LeBron for a beacon of defense as in his NBA career he was usually on the all-defensive team. But his first couple of years coming into the league, he had no interest in playing defense. It made us as fans and media change how we look at talent and where we put our expectations.

Carman continued about how LeBron's talent changed the mind-set of the rest of the rookies getting ready to come to the NBA:

I really do think because of his talent it made us change and temper our expectations for what other talent is going to be. We reference to a guy as saying he is not a LeBron but look what else he can do. It has made us better to look back at it and judge the overall talent of what other players can bring. When you have good talent, you have a chance to win championships, but when you have a good system in place with the talent, you have your best chance to win championships. It has changed for some on how they look at the game and judge talent and how they judge the raw ability.

As LeBron continued to dominate high school courts across the country, the Cavaliers were going through their worst stretch of basketball in the history of the franchise. Heading into the previous 2002–03 off-season, many questions surrounded the upcoming season. The media and fans alike discussed teams potentially tanking the season simply to increase their draft position for a shot at the high school phenomena. The Cavaliers really didn't need to tank anything at that point, as they were already a very low-ranked team. With LeBron being from the Cleveland-Akron area, it seemed like a perfect fit but one that was almost too good to be true to happen for the Cavaliers.

Kenny Roda, legendary Cleveland sports-radio host, knew early on that LeBron would be something special in the NBA one day:

I was one of the first people to jump on the LeBron bandwagon while he was still in high school, after talking with his high school

head coach Dru Joyce, as he told me about LeBron's high basket-
ball IQ. You just looked at the guy physically and mentally, and
he didn't look like a normal high school senior—he looked like a
college senior. So physically and mentally, he was ready. I thought
he would come into the NBA and become the Rookie of the Year and
make an immediate impact!

On July 30, 2002, the Cavaliers traded away their best play-ers, Andre Miller and Bryant Stith, to the Los Angeles Clippers for Harold Jamison and Darius Miles. The move was stunning because it left them without a starting point guard. They would later trade Milt Palacio and sign the free agent point guard Smush Parker. How-ever, none of these players were capable of starting on a regular basis. They had a couple of high-flying scorers with Miles and Ricky Davis, but without a point guard to get them the ball, it was looking like a very long season was ahead for the Cavaliers. This was a clear indi-cation that although the team didn't need to tank forcibly, they were preparing to do so in order to gain the number-one pick of LeBron James. Even more fuel was added to the fire when it was reported that LeBron was allowed to participate in an off-season practice with the Cavaliers. It was unheard of to let a high school student athlete practice with the pros, and it caused head coach John Lucas to be fined as well as suspended for the first two games of the 2002–03 sea-son. Coach Lucas would later admit that he was in a no-win situation and was doing what he was told to do by upper management within the organization.

The Cavaliers opened up the season on the road against the Western Conference powerhouse, the Sacramento Kings. It was a blowout from the very first bounce of the ball. Sacramento exposed the lack of firepower and lack of ability to move the ball by the Cava-liers, holding them to only 67 points. The final score was 94–67, and the game looked as bad, as the final score demonstrated. And without a starting point guard, it didn't appear that the Cavaliers would be improving anytime soon. It was a clear indication of how the entire rest of the season would go for the team. They were set up to suffer and prepared to let their fans also suffer as they plotted for the arrival of the Chosen One.

Following that opening night, the Cavaliers continued in their downward spiral with a 15-game losing streak. By December, their record was 6–24, with no improvement in sight. Things didn't get much better after that, and by the all-star break, John Lucas was fired as head coach. He left the team with an 8–34 record. In just over a season and a half as coach, Lucas barely led the team to a paltry 37 wins. Additionally, the franchise was going through some serious growing pains.

Cavaliers assistant coach Keith Smart took over as head coach, replacing John Lucas, but he didn't have any better luck, as the team finished the season tied with the Denver Nuggets for the worst record in the league at 17–65. It was the Cavaliers fifth straight season missing the playoffs, and the team had gone through four head coach changes in that same period of time. This instability was very uncharacteristic for a Gordon Gund–owned team, and he was on the lookout for change to arrive quickly.

The silver lining in the dark cloud of that season was the fact that Žydrūnas Ilgauskas played in 81 games—a great sign that he had fully recovered from years of foot injuries and surgeries. Ilgauskas was so impressive that year that he was voted onto the Eastern Conference All-Star Team. He averaged 17.2 points a game, along with 7.5 rebounds. He also led the team in blocks with 1.9 a night. For the Cavaliers to improve, the physical health of Ilgauskas would come to be a vital component of the overall effectiveness of the team. He solidified the frontcourt and served as a key player for a number of years to come. Additionally, the impact of the friendship that Ilgauskas would go on to have with LeBron 11 years later would also prove vital to future success the team.

Equally impressive was the play of rookie standout Carlos Boozer. He played in 81 games, averaging 10 points a night and a strong 7.5 rebounds per game. The dream of Boozer in the frontcourt ripping down rebounds and scoring points looked bright for the Cavaliers, as he was quickly shaping up into a major player that the Cavaliers hoped to be able to count on to be their starting power forward for a long time to come.

The 2003 NBA draft was regarded as one of the strongest in history. The top five picks produced four of the best players currently playing today. Cleveland selected LeBron James with their number-one pick; two picks later, Denver selected future all-star Carmelo Anthony from Syracuse. The Toronto Raptors selected Chris Bosh—one of the top players in the game today—out of Georgia Tech with the fourth pick. The fifth pick went to the Miami Heat, who struck gold with their selection of Dwayne Wade. (The Heat would eventually combine Wade with Shaquille O'Neal and win the NBA Championship just three years later.) The draft was loaded with talent, but it was clear that Cleveland was receiving its top prize.

Opening night for LeBron took place on the West Coast when the Cleveland Cavaliers visited the Sacramento Kings; he scored 25 points against them and set an NBA record for the most points scored by a prep-to-pro player in his debut outing. The Cavaliers lost the game 106–82—the team couldn't do much to help LeBron and couldn't stop the high-powered Sacramento attack. Fans in Cleveland and the world over didn't mind staying up late to watch LeBron's professional debut. With the final score not in Cleveland's favor, it was a very promising sign that LeBron was not discouraged and still put together a fine opening-night effort.

Despite LeBron's playing well, the Cavaliers lost their first five games of the season before winning back-to-back games at home against Washington and New York. As a rookie, LeBron handled the pressure of his position well. The team, however, did not, enduring an eight-game losing streak from late November through early December. Davis and Miles spent their court time hogging the ball when they really needed to find a way to hand the ball off to LeBron. On Monday, January 12, 2004, the Cavaliers hit a new season low of 15 games under 500. It was then that the winning combination of LeBron and Boozer began to form. LeBron showed great improvement during his first year and instantly became the team leader. Without the negative influence of Miles and Davis controlling the team, the other young players were able to grow together and make drastic and encouraging strides in the right direction. The writing was on the wall for Miles and Davis.

The Cavaliers rattled off several winning streaks, including a seven-game clip in early March that put them in the playoff hunt. In a late-season match-up with the New Jersey Nets, LeBron scored a season-high 41 points—becoming the youngest player, at age 19, in league history to score at least 40 points in a game. Not only were the great plays of LeBron helping the team, but a couple of key midseason trades by general manager Jim Paxson helped as well.

In a second-round draft pick, the Cavaliers traded Davis, Chris Mihm, and Michael Stewart to the Boston Celtics for Tony Battie, Kedrick Brown, and Eric Williams. The team later decided to also trade Miles to the Portland Trail Blazers for Jeff McInnis. It was a clear sign that with LeBron leading the team, all selfish ball-hogs had to go—with Miles and Davis at the top of the list. McInnis was a key pickup, as he could shoot and pass while providing instant offense every time he touched the ball. Williams was another important addition who brought a certain sense of veteran leadership to the team.

Despite the added support, the Cavaliers would go on to tire out late in the season and slump through a seven-game losing streak in the final weeks. The team did close out the year strong, however, with three straight wins despite already being eliminated from playoff contention.

Finishing with averages of 20.9 points, 5.5 rebounds, and 5.9 assists per game, LeBron went on to be named the NBA Rookie of the Year for the 2003–04 season—the first Cavalier in history to receive the designation—joining Oscar Robertson and Michael Jordan as the only players in NBA history to average at least 20 points, 5 rebounds, and 5 assists per game in their rookie year. LeBron played in 79 of the 82 games that season, demonstrating his durability as a player despite his very physical style of play.

Jerry Mires, host of *The Sports Fix* on IHeartRadio, provided his take on LeBron coming into the league:

I sensed when he was in the ninth grade that he would have the impact on the NBA one day that he did. We all knew! He was raised to be an NBA player. He was 10 years old when people around him figured it out and changed the course of his life because they knew what he was meant to become. I don't think anyone was surprised at his total and utter domination at such a young age of all competition that stood in his path.

Roda wasn't surprised either with LeBron's dominant first season in the league:

His rookie year was better than anyone else ever coming out of high school and better than any of us have seen or even expected. He deserved to be the 2003–04 Rookie of the Year. He even exceeded my hopes for him. He went out and did better than anyone's expectations. It was an incredible thing to witness firsthand.

11

In the 2004 off-season, Drew Gooden was brought in to fill the void at power forward left behind by Carlos Boozer. He was a former fourth overall pick in the 2002 NBA draft by the Memphis Grizzlies. The hopes for Gooden were high after a great college career at Kansas. In 2002, he led the league in rebounds and was named the National Association of Basketball Coaches National Player of the Year. The Jayhawks went 33–4, including 16–0 in the Big 12 Conference play to win against Kansas—its first conference championship since 1998. Gooden had two forgetful years with both the Memphis Grizzlies and the Orlando Magic, and he hoped to turn things around with the Cavaliers.

LeBron picked up where he had left off the year before and started his second season red-hot. He once again led the team in all offensive categories and was good enough to be voted as a starter in the All-Star Game for the Eastern Conference. Sadly, the team couldn't turn the corner and missed the playoffs again, despite winning 42 games. They also went through an ownership change when Dan Gilbert bought the team from Gordon Gund. Gilbert's first move was to fire head coach Paul Silas. It was a sign of things to come that Gilbert wasn't afraid of making changes for the benefit of the team.

The upcoming summer would go a long way in shaping the future of the team. A new coach and general manager were hired, and for the first time, getting to play with LeBron James was used as a bargaining chip to bring in new talent. The only question that remained was the same one that would always stand out during LeBron's time as a Cavalier: Could the team find the help it needed?

CHAPTER TWO

The Next Level

The Cavaliers had narrowly missed the playoffs, and the team's next move needed to be landing the right head coach. LeBron showed he could play at an elite caliber level, but he needed the right team around him with the best head coach to guide them in order to achieve national championship success. Former player Danny Ferry returned to Cleveland to become the general manager, and his biggest move was signing new head coach Mike Brown.

Kenny Roda gave his input on why Mike Brown was chosen to be the next head coach to lead LeBron and the Cavaliers:

Number one, Dan Gilbert was impatient, and I think he will admit that now. I liked Paul Silas and thought he was from the old school and taught things to LeBron James that only an old-school guy could teach. Mike Brown was coming from an organization in the San Antonio Spurs where they were the model team many teams wanted to structure themselves after because of the success that they had. Mike Brown was a defensive-minded coach from Gregg Popovich's system and organization, and if you're not going to hire a retread coach, then you're going hire the young, up-and-coming assistant from a good program, and that is exactly what Mike Brown was. Dan Gilbert felt that with Mike Brown being around Popovich and watching him handle the likes of Tim Duncan, Tony Parker, Manu Ginóbili, and players like that, based on his pedigree and his work ethic and ability to learn from Gregg Popovich, that put Mike Brown at the top of the Cavaliers wish list, and that is why they went after him so hard. Danny Ferry also had something to do with it and spent time in San Antonio as well. Danny Ferry knew of Mike and the Popovich way, so you can connect the dots there. A new owner, with Danny Ferry the new GM coming from San Antonio, and it kind of just fit the needs of the Cavaliers at that time.

Mike Brown began his basketball career as an unpaid video intern with the Denver Nuggets. He would spend five years as their video coordinator. Then Brown went on to spend time on the coaching staffs of the Washington Wizards and San Antonio Spurs. Brown was with San Antonio when they won their NBA Championship in 2003. It was different then, the life of fame and high expectations that LeBron had for the last 10 years. For the Cavaliers fans, it would be interesting to see if the two personalities would mesh. Mike Brown was used to being around a team-oriented style of offense and not relying on just one superstar player. To his credit, as the years went on, LeBron was seen as the ultimate team player and one who made the players around him much better. Perhaps it was the best of both worlds for Mike Brown that his first coaching gig would have the game's best up-and-coming player to lead it, and any playoff spot would be seen as an immediate impact in the right direction.

Ken Carman, radio host of 92.3 The Fan, provided his thoughts on why they brought Mike Brown in:

I think they brought him in because of the shared time that he had in San Antonio. A lot of guys—and we do this a lot, because he was an assistant for a great coach—we falsely assume he is going to be great. Mike Brown may have been a great assistant coach, but he was not ready for an NBA head coaching spot at that time. If Mike Brown was a college coach and had players listening to his every word, I think he would do very well at that level as a head coach. He really is a good guy with a lot of good things about him, and I think that when you have players listen to him the way they would have to in college I think he would do very well, much better than he did at the pro level. In the pros, this isn't the Bill Fitch era anymore or the Red Auerbach era—now these players have egos. You have 12 different players with 12 egos and personalities to handle. There are a lot of guys that you have to rein in, and there is a pecking order, clearly. One of Mike Brown's greatest challenges would be reining in the egos of players such as LeBron James and Kobe Bryant in his career.

Jerry Mires supplied his input on the hiring of Coach Brown:

A lot of it was because he was connected to that system, that San Antonio–type system that Dan Gilbert is in love with—the no-superstar type of thing. Paul Silas to me was the right kind of coach for LeBron James because he puts the hammer down, no offense to Austin Carr. I think that's what the problem was. He wanted to make LeBron James pay his dues; there is a real thing to that no matter how great someone is at something. They still have to earn it—even if doesn't take them long and it is not very hard for them—they still have to earn it. If the player doesn't earn it, then they don't respect the coach. Mike Brown was a great coach, I liked him, [but] a lot of people don't because of his offensive skill set with coaching. The problem was that he was dead in the water the second he said, "I'm lucky LeBron James lets me coach him!" The minute you say that, you're done, man! Unfortunately, the whole NBA has become a caterer-to-one-player-on-each-team sort of thing, which is terrible for the sport. If you don't cater to them, the coach gets fired because an owner isn't going to move the star out. Trust me, if LeBron James doesn't like a coach, then he's gone. I'm not saying that superstars run the team, but LeBron James pretty much does.

Danny Ferry wanted to bring the best talent to Cleveland, but after premier players such as Ray Allen, and Michael Redd signed elsewhere, he had to settle for B-level free agents Larry Hughes, Donyell Marshall, and Damon Jones. Despite not getting the top-tier free agents, the Cavaliers were expected to compete fiercely for a play-off spot that 2005–06 season.

Larry Hughes tasted success early in his basketball career when he was playing for Christian Brothers College High School, leading his teammates in a winning effort for the Missouri state championship in 1997. From high school, Hughes went to play only one season of college basketball at Saint Louis University. He performed well in his one and only college season, averaging 20.9 points, 5.1 rebounds, 2.4 assists, and 2.16 steals. He was St. Louis University's best player and led the Billikens to the NCAA tournament that year, making it to the second round of 32 teams after a win over the University of Massachusetts before getting knocked out of the competition. It was still a strong showing for the smaller school. He was named Freshman of the Year and had some pre-draft hype as he was selected by the Philadelphia 76ers in the first-round pick of the 1998 NBA draft. The main reason the Cavaliers wanted to sign him in free agency was that he was known for being a versatile and athletic guard with strong defensive abilities—the perfect fit for Mike Brown's system.

As Hughes bounced around from team to team in the NBA because of his inconsistent offense, it was his defense that kept him in starting lineups. He was selected to the 2004–05 NBA All-Defensive First Team as a member of the Washington Wizards, where he led the league in steals per game with an average of 2.89. Many were surprised, however, when Hughes signed a five-year, $70 million contract with the Cleveland Cavaliers as a free agent in the summer of 2005. Many feel that it was a clear sign of desperation as they searched for veteran help of any kind for LeBron, and after Ray Allen and Michael Redd both passed, Hughes was the next best remaining free agent out there. He did average 16.2 points and 37.6 minutes per game. Hughes was generally seen as a nice guy by many reporters in the local Cleveland media upon his arrival, and later on he received the inaugural Austin Carr Good Guy Award, which recognizes the Cavaliers player who is most cooperative with and understanding of the media, the community, and the public.

Unlike Hughes, Damon Jones was an undrafted free agent after playing three years in college with the University of Houston Cougars. Before arriving in Cleveland, he had never played with the same team for more than one season. He was coming off the best season of his career with the Miami Heat, where he set career highs in games started, minutes played, field goals made and attempted, field goal percentage, three-point field goals made and attempted, three-point field goal percentage, free throws made and attempted, rebounds, steals, blocked shots, and points scored. His 225 three-point field goals was third best in the NBA, and his three-point field goal percentage was fifth best that season. He also scored in double figures on 48 occasions. The main attraction of bringing in Jones was his playoff experience playing with Shaquille O'Neal and Dwyane Wade, as he had played in 15 playoff games, averaging 12.1 points and 4 assists, and shot 42.9 percent from the three-point range. Jones decided to leave Miami and signed a four-year contract for $16.1 million with the Cleveland Cavaliers on September 8, 2005. Sadly for Damon Jones and the Cavaliers, many in the local media and fans alike saw his time in Cleveland as a failure. Roda would often refer to him as "Amon Ones," with no D and no J, meaning that Jones couldn't shoot or play defense. Many others felt the same way as Roda.

The new coach and key free-agent pickups worked well for the team, as they brought a 31–21 record into the All-Star Game and were clearly one of the league's most improved teams. LeBron took his place as one of the best players in the game: He won the Most Valuable Player award in the All-Star Game, scoring 29 points with 6 assists and becoming the youngest player to ever win the award. He also led the Eastern Conference to a double-digit come-from-behind victory. The Cavaliers remained hot under LeBron's incredible playing and went on another nine-game winning streak before the season ended. The team finished with 50 wins for the first time in years, and LeBron was about to enter the NBA playoffs for the first time with one of the hottest teams in basketball by his side. It was an incredible turnaround for a franchise that had only won 17 games just three years prior. Coach Brown had brought the Cavaliers to the playoffs in his first season as coach, and it looked as though general manager Danny Ferry was making all the right moves with his young team led by the league's best and brightest rising superstar.

The Cavaliers' first-round playoff opponents were the Washington Wizards, led by a trio of superstars: Antawn Jamison, Gilbert Arenas, and Caron Butler. The Wizards were the fifth seed and seen as a sharp first challenge for the LeBron-led Cleveland Cavaliers. LeBron was coming off his best season as a pro, and many wondered how he would handle the pressure of his first playoff series. The 21-year-old LeBron ended all doubts in game one, scoring 32 points with 11 assists and 11 rebounds en route to a triple-double. The wunderkind's terrific effort was more than enough to lead the Cavaliers to a 97–86 victory. LeBron was later quoted after the game as saying, "It's a God-given talent. I don't know how the box score will end up at the end of the game. I just try to go out there and play my game." This quote showed that LeBron was a team player focused on doing whatever he could to help the team win and not focus on his own statistics.

The "big three" of Washington were too much for Cleveland to handle—they dropped game two 89–84 to even up the series. Game three took place in Washington, and LeBron again displayed a masterful performance. The Cleveland Cavaliers trailed all game but used an incredible 14-point fourth quarter effort from LeBron to come from behind and win 97–96. LeBron scored 41 total points and hit the game-winning shot with 5.7 seconds remaining in the game. It was apparent not only to Cleveland but also to the basketball world that LeBron was quickly becoming unstoppable. Coach Brown summed it up perfectly when he said, "LeBron James is special." It was short but extremely accurate.

LeBron followed his stellar game-three effort with another impressive performance in game four by scoring 38 points. It wasn't enough, however: He didn't get much help from his teammates, and the Wizards won 106–96, once again tying the series.

Game five returned the series to Cleveland. The dramatic back-and-forth series was quickly becoming a classic, and this game did not disappoint. The game remained tied after four hard-fought quarters. As overtime began, the fans in attendance at the Quicken Loans Arena could sense another dramatic conclusion. Gilbert Arenas made two pressure-packed foul shots to put the Wizards ahead with only 3.9 seconds left in overtime. Mike Brown called time-out, and the Cavaliers drew up the final play. LeBron received the inbound pass and cut to the hole with enough time to lay in a game-winning shot over Washington defender Michael Ruffin. It was LeBron's second game winner of the series, capped off with a 45-point performance.

Cavaliers fans and basketball fans worldwide began to realize they were witnessing something truly special.

Game six returned to Washington with the Cavaliers on the brink of advancing to the next round of the playoffs. This game, just like game five, went into overtime. Washington had led throughout the majority of the game, and the Cavaliers used a strong second half to force overtime. Anderson Varejão had double-digit rebounds, Hughes chipped in with 12 assists, and LeBron had 35 points, but the key points came from backup shooting guard Damon Jones. With 4.8 seconds left in overtime and the Cavaliers down one, Jones' jump shot put the Cavaliers into the Eastern Conference semi-finals against the Detroit Pistons. It was a huge win for the Cleveland Cavaliers and another magical moment in a classic series.

Few people outside of Cleveland gave the Cavaliers any chance at defeating the top-seeded Detroit Pistons. Through the first two games it looked like the skeptics were correct, as the Pistons handled the Cavaliers with ease, winning both games held at the Palace of Auburn Hills. With the series returning to Cleveland for game three, the Cavaliers were desperate for a victory—and that's just what they got. LeBron had another triple-double with 21 points, 10 rebounds, and 10 assists to push Cleveland back into the series. LeBron was proving to be a clutch player when they needed him the most.

For the second straight game, the Cavaliers were without a starting shooting guard because Hughes was mourning the loss of his brother, Justin, who had passed away earlier in the week. The Cavaliers played hard for their teammate, using a gritty defensive effort to beat the Pistons 74–72 and even the series. The team used Hughes's family situation to become stronger as a team and grow together as men. They were a team united—and suddenly a real threat to upset the defending two-time Eastern Conference Champion Detroit Pistons.

Game five returned to the Palace of Auburn Hills, with Detroit looking to reclaim the series lead in front of the team's hometown fans. The Cavaliers used a 32-point effort by LeBron to upset the Pistons 86–84. LeBron again showed his ability to make those around him better by finding power forward Drew Gooden with 27 seconds left, allowing Gooden to hit the shot that put Cleveland ahead for good. LeBron was quoted by the Cleveland *Plain Dealer* after the game as saying, "They aren't the Big Bad Wolf and we aren't the Three Little Pigs. We are all grown men and we know we can beat them!"

Detroit was able to use late offensive rebounds by Rip Hamilton in game six to steal the victory and force a game seven. The Cavaliers played miserably in game seven and were defeated 79–61, ending their magical playoff run. It was a disappointing end, but it showed that, if given another chance, LeBron could lead the Cavaliers deeper into the playoffs. He proved he could make game-winning shots when called upon and also set up his teammates. He had answered many questions, but one of the biggest ones would now arise: Could LeBron get past the Detroit Pistons? It was the same exact question that his idol Michael Jordan once had to face and, like his idol, LeBron's best days were yet to come!

*LeBron James drove past the Detroit Pistons on his way to the
2007 NBA Finals.*   Photo: Tom Culp

CHAPTER THREE

Beating Detroit and the NBA Finals

T he 2006–07 season was a roller-coaster ride that, ironically, had Cleveland achieving a record identical to that of the previous season: 50–32. What was different was that this season, their record qualified them for a second seed in the playoffs instead of a fourth seed. This also meant that the Cavaliers would be on the opposite side of the bracket with the Detroit Pistons, and a potential rematch would not take place until the Eastern Conference Finals.

LeBron continued to improve. By the end of the season, he had finished with a 27.3-point average, along with averaging 6.7 rebounds and 6 assists per game. He was seen as one of the top five players in the league in only his fourth season in pro basketball. The first-round playoff series was a rematch against the Washington Wizards. The result was far different from the previous season's dramatic series: Cleveland swept the Wizards under the rug with ease in four straight games. LeBron continued to dominate, and the Cavaliers made quick work of the Wizards.

Round two would be a tougher task, because the team was up against Jason Kidd, Vince Carter, Richard Jefferson, and the much-improved New Jersey Nets. The Cavaliers won game one with ease, and

LeBron's 36-point effort in game two enabled them to roll past New Jersey and take a 2–0 series lead. New Jersey bounced back at home, though, and won game three to climb back in the series.

In game four, Hughes chipped in 19 points alongside LeBron's 30 to secure a narrow 87–85 victory against New Jersey. Two games later, Cleveland finished New Jersey off in the series, 4–2, advancing to the Eastern Conference Championship series to once again play the Detroit Pistons.

Game one in Detroit ended in dramatic fashion, as LeBron had a chance to put Cleveland ahead in the closing seconds but instead opted to pass off to teammate Donyell Marshall, who promptly missed a three-pointer to give Detroit the win. LeBron would undergo extreme criticism following the game for not taking the shot. Marshall had hit 6 three-pointers in game six of the semifinals, clinching the win against New Jersey a few nights prior, and LeBron saw that Marshall was wide open for the shot. Despite playing the Pistons tough all night and holding a lead numerous times, the Cavaliers still lost game one 79–76.

Game two would follow almost the exact storyline as the previous night. Once again, the game came down to the end with Cleveland having the ball and a chance to win. This time, however, LeBron didn't hesitate to drive the lane and try to take the game-winning shot. He was fouled hard by numerous Detroit Pistons, only the referees chose not to call it, and the Detroit Pistons eventually got the rebound, ending Cleveland's chance. The Detroit Pistons made some foul shots after Coach Brown's technical penalty for arguing the fouls on LeBron not being called. Brown was livid, and he had every right to be, as the Detroit Pistons were hammering LeBron every time he touched the ball. The final score matched game one, with the Detroit Pistons on top 79–76.

The Cavaliers used their anger and heartbreak from both of the close losses to come out hungry and aggressive in game three back in Cleveland. The series continued to be physical, but the Cavaliers fought hard and won games three and four to even up the series. This series was following a timeline identical to the previous year's, and game five was setting up to be every bit as crucial and dramatic. Cleveland again showed the willingness and strength not to break despite being down 2–0 in the series as they had the year before. It was another sign that LeBron's dominance gave the Cavaliers momentum and confidence despite how bleak a situation looked. As long as LeBron was on the roster, the Cavaliers and their fans knew that the team had a chance to win any game and any series. A player with the heart, hustle, and determination that LeBron carries with him every time his feet touch the court is unstoppable.

Game five of the Eastern Conference Finals took place on May 31, 2007, and thanks to LeBron it would go down as one of the greatest games of all time. In one of the best playoff efforts in the history of the game, LeBron scored his team's last 25 points to lead the Cavaliers to a 109–107 double overtime victory. LeBron scored 29 of his team's last 30 points, and the Pistons had no answer for him. NBA fans everywhere sat in awe as he singlehandedly took the game over late in the fourth quarter and carried his teammates to the game-five win.

Ken Carman offered his insight on that epic night for LeBron and the Cavaliers:

I look back on it now, seven years later, and can truly appreciate what he did. It becomes even more remarkable when you look at his weak supporting cast—names like Damon Jones, Drew Gooden, Larry Hughes, Eric Snow, Donyell Marshall, Ira Newble, and Boobie Gibson. Let's be honest: These guys were a collection of garbage, with the exception of Anderson. It was just a total collection of garbage trying to support LeBron James. As we look back on it, I can't defend that rotation and entire roster around him. They tried and made an effort at it, and I know that Larry Hughes was battling family problems with his brother dying, but he didn't seem to care about basketball before or after that during his time in Cleveland; he even admitted as much. Years later, you saw the collapse of Mo Williams in the playoffs around LeBron James. This is why it is important for them to go out and get veteran talent like Mike Miller, Ray Allen, and James Jones like they did when [LeBron] left for Miami. He bases it on trust; he truly tries to trust his teammates. There is a difference between LeBron James and Kobe Bryant, and it isn't just rings. Kobe trusts no one but Kobe. We call Kobe a ball hog, but I just think he has trust issues. For LeBron James, it's different because I think he trusts too much. He passed it off too much at times because he trusted his teammates too much. He took a lot of heat for it because he was the one with all the talent and should have been taking the shots and have the ball in his hands during the final seconds. It's important, however, for him to have other players he can pass it to when he is being double-covered. When you look back at that team as time goes on, we really marvel at what he has done. When you have a complete team like the Detroit Pistons who are coached by a great coach in Flip Saunders, it took a Herculean effort by LeBron James to get them past Detroit.

Kenny Roda, who was also on hand to witness that night live, gave his impressions on LeBron's incredible performance:

I was at the Palace of Auburn Hills that night in Detroit to witness it. I watched it in person and could not believe my eyes what I was witnessing that day. You talk about being in a zone and you hear athletes talk about being in a zone, and that was the ultimate example of being in the zone. I think it was 25 straight and 29 of the last 30 and it was just amazing. He was doing it with jumpers, with men in his face that couldn't stop him. He was driving to the basket and throwing down on guys like Chris Webber, Rasheed Wallace, and company, it was just something to behold. We were sitting there wondering how much more can he do and then he just kept giving more and more. He was exhausted when it was over, just exhausted walking off the court that night. They won that game and then won again in game six to advance. It was one of the most incredible performances of any individual basketball player I have ever seen. I put it up there with Magic Johnson going 42–15–7 in the final game against the 76ers in 1980 when Kareem Abdul-Jabbar was out of the lineup to win the Lakers the championship. Those games stand out in my mind as two of the best games I have ever witnessed based on the impact. They were playoff games and very important contests. It was the greatest game I have ever witnessed in person as far as a playoff game. To this day, am I blessed to have been in that building on that historic evening. I got to watch LeBron James put on a show that, in my opinion, hasn't been duplicated in a Cavaliers uniform or many uniforms around the NBA.

Jerry Mires also recalled the epic game fondly:

That was amazing! That was one of the most amazing things and performances I have ever seen in any sport during any generation in the history of sports in the United States of America and all the galaxies combined. It was just out of this world! I'm a LeBron James critic in a lot of ways, but that was just like basketball at its highest form! It was like some of those moments over the years that you see with guys like MJ and Larry Bird, where they just take a game over. LeBron James just took it over and dominated—he just refused to lose. That was basketball at its highest form, that run right there!

The Detroit Pistons focused all of their efforts during the game-six battle on trying to stop LeBron. They held him in modest check through the beginning of the game, but it would only be a matter of time before LeBron broke loose. With the Pistons' attention elsewhere, it allowed rookie sensation Daniel "Boobie" Gibson to get open for several three-pointers. By the night's end, Gibson had hit 5 three-pointers on his way to a game high of 31 points. The plan on focusing solely on LeBron exploded in the face of Detroit and allowed Gibson to come out red-hot, eventually leading Cleveland to the series-clinching win.

Roda also provided his impression of the clinching performance from Gibson and the Cavaliers: "It was Boobie who really went off that night. LeBron James' numbers were good, but he was so exhausted from the incredible game five that it had a carry-over effect and Boobie Gibson was there to pick up the slack in game number six."

Despite the outcome in the NBA Finals—a sweep by the San Antonio Spurs—the run of the Cleveland Cavaliers in the 2007 playoffs will always be remembered as the coming-out party for LeBron. Carman gave his reasons as to why they couldn't get past San Antonio in the finals: "The San Antonio Spurs were a complete team full of great shooters being coached by a legendary coach in Gregg Popovich. They played great team basketball. It is humbling, but it shows you what to do as a measuring stick on how to reach that next level. In a team sport like basketball you have to be humble and not let one guy take over." In a matter of four years the Cavaliers had managed to rebound from having the league's worst record to reaching the NBA Finals. It was a remarkable turnaround, and now the only question remaining was not if they could get back to the finals, but when they did, could they win it all?

CHAPTER FOUR

Acquiring Talent for LeBron

It was a quiet off-season. The team signed only one free agent of note: Devin Brown, a five-year veteran who had spent time with San Antonio, Denver, Utah, and New Orleans. He was a solid backup shooting guard, and with Larry Hughes's injury concerns, the Cavaliers needed to have a reliable backup. The night before the opening game, the team received some good news: They had come to terms on a contract extension with Sasha Pavlović, who was holding out at the time. He would not be ready for the first few games but would return to action in time for their six-game West Coast road trip only a few days away. Cleveland got off to a slow start with the holdout of Anderson and an injury that kept LeBron out for seven games. It was looking as though a return to the finals would be a much harder and longer journey than the prior season.

The Cavaliers were still struggling to find their stride and slumped into a 14–17 record as the calendar turned to 2008. It was at this point that the team finally snapped out of its coma and got hot, eventually turning it around and achieving a winning record later into the season. As the Cavaliers entered into the last week of

February with a 30–24 record, there had been rumors for a while that the Cavaliers chemistry wasn't as good as prior years and that a major shake-up could happen. Despite the winning record, general manager Danny Ferry still felt that the team needed a change in order to return to the later rounds of the playoffs.

On February 21, 2008, Danny Ferry pulled off a blockbuster that no one saw coming. He took part in a three-team trade with the Chicago Bulls and Seattle SuperSonics that would change 25 percent of the Cavaliers' roster. As part of a three-team trade, the Cleveland Cavaliers traded Donyell Marshall and Ira Newble to the Seattle SuperSonics and sent Shannon Brown, Drew Gooden, Larry Hughes, and Cedric Simmons to the Chicago Bulls; the Chicago Bulls traded Joe Smith, Ben Wallace, and a 2009 second-round draft pick (Danny Green was later selected) to the Cleveland Cavaliers; the Chicago Bulls traded Adrian Griffin to the Seattle SuperSonics; and the Seattle SuperSonics traded Wally Szczerbiak and Delonte West to the Cleveland Cavaliers. It was a crucial trade that brought on high risk but also the chance for a very high reward.

Roda explained why it was crucial for the trade to happen and his belief regarding why it occurred:

> *They had to bring in some veterans. They were coming in off of a season where they had been beaten in four straight games in the NBA Finals against the San Antonio Spurs. Even though some of the games were close, they needed to tweak the roster since they were already figuring out how to try and keep LeBron James as a player in Cleveland. So when you're doing whatever you can to make him happy and make the team better, you need those two things in concert and have to do both if you want to get it done. They were trying to show him that they were going to do everything that they possibly could to make the Cavaliers a championship team and keep them at that level. I give Danny Ferry all the credit in the world. Was it the*

greatest trade? Clearly no, because they didn't win a championship. But Danny Ferry had the pressure of trying to find the best deals out there to improve the Cavs chances of winning and also keep LeBron James. Danny was doing his job as a general manager to bring in the most talent he could to maintain the level of play for the Cavaliers at a championship level and keep LeBron James happy, so that is why he went all in. I give Danny Ferry a lot of credit—instead of just standing by and doing nothing, hoping that they would get back there again, they went all in. It didn't work out, but I at least appreciate a general manager [who] if he's going to go down, he's going to go down swinging. Danny tried numerous times to get the right pieces and parts to make this a championship team. Unfortunately, they were unable to get back to the finals that season.

Carman also gave his thoughts on the big trade:

When you look at it now, that was the beginning of them trying to see what is going to be in the future. I have always thought that LeBron was so young that at this point, they were trying to see who they could bring in to please him. Now there is a difference in the resolve of LeBron that there wasn't back then. We were already wondering if we could hold on to him, and he very much let that go on. He catered to those who believed he would leave for New York or Los Angeles. I think that there was a little bit of distrust in what he was going to do. You were hanging your hat on LeBron and wondering what he was going to do from time to time. You just tried to make him as comfortable as possible and make some moves to try and help him. It was to see if he could really help himself because he wasn't willing to sign a long-term deal. Well, if you're not willing to sign a long-term deal in your early 20s, why would big-name free agents come here to play with him and want to sign a long-term deal to play with him? There was too much of a chance of the rug being pulled out from other free agents if he left. Let's be honest! Years later when he did leave, players like Mo Williams were upset, because he knew that he had to stay on a team that wouldn't be good without LeBron. That's just how these guys think. It is not an anti-fan thing or anything like that. It's an opportunity-being taken-from-them type of thing. There are some real hurt feelings there. There's always that "what if" players have in the back of their mind. I don't think Danny Ferry was willing to make other moves because of trust issues. I think we were saving too much not to make moves until then because we were getting too farsighted and not enough nearsighted. I think it was too little too late with some of the pieces they got.

It was a gutsy move by Ferry, but one he had to make to strengthen the team for another run deep into the playoffs. Hughes had been too injury prone and inconsistent, making him expendable. He wasn't the solid number-two scoring threat that they had needed him to be when they signed him to the large free-agent deal in the summer of 2005. Drew Gooden had never quite reached his potential many thought he had when he was picked fourth in the draft several years earlier. Gooden was loved by the fans and his teammates, but Ferry knew that the trade wouldn't be possible unless he included Gooden in it.

Mires believed that Delonte West was the key part of that deal:

Delonte West was the key of that trade. I realize people like to make snarky Delonte West jokes, but he was the key in that trade. Shaq O'Neal even said he would play anytime with Delonte West because he has that dog in him. He's just a street fighter . . . that hungry player who's going to fight for everything that you have. He is the kind of guy that when you're in a dark alley, I'd rather have him covering your back than a 10-foot giant. He was so key, just look at the difference that last season after he fell apart—that was a big part of the reason the Cavs struggled at times in 2010. Not just legal problems, but he struggled with mental problems as well. He was sick with bipolar and other issues.

The team reacted well to the new cast of players, as the Cavaliers won the first seven of nine games after the trade. It was going to take time to mesh, but the new players showed they were hungry to play well and contribute right away. They finished the regular season at 45–37 and looked poised for another run at the Eastern Conference Championship.

The Cavaliers' first-round opponent was a familiar foe: the Washington Wizards. It would be the third straight season the team had to face Washington in the opening round. The Wizards had their "Big Three" ready with Gilbert Arenas, Caron Butler, and Antawn Jamison poised to do everything they could not to get beat again. The Cavaliers were ready for the Wizards to come out strong and fight them hard the entire game. In the end it took a 32-point performance by LeBron, and the Cavaliers took game one 93–86. The Wizards had led after the first and third quarters, but the Cavaliers used a 28-point fourth quarter to overcome them for good. West helped out with 16 points in his first playoff game as a Cavalier and also chipped in with 5 rebounds, 2 steals, and 5 assists.

Game two was not nearly as close, and the Cavaliers blew out the Wizards 116–86. It was a 30-point victory that proved how good Cleveland could be when running on all four cylinders. LeBron had another incredible night with 30 points, 12 assists, 2 blocked shots, and 9 rebounds. It was an impressive night for The King. Wally Szczerbiak hit 2 three-pointers on his way to a 15-point night. He was starting at shooting guard while West ran the point. They would travel to Washington with a commanding 2–0 lead in the best-of-seven series.

Washington returned the favor in game three and blew out the Cavaliers at home by a score of 108–72. LeBron had 22 points, but only one other player was able to score in double digits. It was a poor effort that allowed Washington back into the series. LeBron would need more support from his surrounding cast if they were going to do anything in the playoffs.

Game four was a back-and-forth affair that would come down to the wire once again. The Wizards held a four-point lead after the first quarter of action. The Cavaliers outscored them in the second quarter 30–16 to take a 10-point lead into halftime. Washington cut into the lead in the third quarter and only trailed by seven heading into the fourth. The gamed continued to be close, but in the end the Cavaliers managed to hang on for a 100–97 win. It gave the team a stranglehold on the series heading back home for game five.

This game was another impressive effort by LeBron, as he scored 34 points, 12 rebounds, 7 assists, and 2 steals. He was becoming an unstoppable monster in the playoffs once again. West also showed that he could be a great number-two scoring threat behind LeBron, chipping in with 21 points, 5 assists, and 3 steals. Game five back in Cleveland saw Washington slip by with a razor-thin win of 88–87. LeBron scored with ease again, finishing with 34 points and pulling down 10 rebounds. The effort by LeBron was amazing but not enough, and the series was headed back to Washington for game six.

Washington used a 31-point first quarter at home in game six to take an early four-point lead. The Cavaliers held the Washington offense in check in the second quarter, allowing only 17 points and taking a 56–48 lead into halftime. They were only 24 minutes away from reaching the next round, and they came out of the half with the full intent on shutting Washington down for good. The Cavaliers outscored the Wizards 23–16 and took a 15-point lead heading into the final frame. Washington managed to cut into the lead a tiny bit, but the

Cavaliers were just too much to overcome and won the game 105–88. Cleveland was headed back to the Eastern Conference Semi-Finals for the third straight year.

The game six–clinching win was highlighted by a 27-point scoring effort from LeBron and 26 points scored by Szczerbiak, including an incredible 6 three-pointers that broke the spirit of Washington and its fans. Gibson also scored 22 points off the bench, including 4 three-pointers of his own. The Cavaliers would need the momentum and positive energy to continue, as they were about to face the team with the NBA's best record in the next round: the Boston Celtics.

With the major acquisitions of perennial all-stars Kevin Garnett and Ray Allen in the off-season, the Boston Celtics finished the season with a record of 66–16 and posted the best single-season turnaround in NBA history, improving by 42 wins from the previous season. Garnett was named NBA Defensive Player of the Year, while NBA executive Danny Ainge, who had executed what was deemed as "the most dramatic NBA turnaround ever," was named NBA Executive of the Year. With Paul Pierce already on the roster of the Boston Celtics, Garnett, Ray, and Pierce became known as the new "Big Three." The Celtics were the first team to form a super group of talent in free agency and trade. The Celtics also had a highly talented rookie point guard from Kentucky, Rajon Rondo.

The Cavaliers were going to have their work cut out for them, because Boston was heavily favored to win the NBA Championship that year. The Celtics were coming off of a surprisingly grueling seven-game series against the Atlanta Hawks, where the Hawks shocked everyone by pushing Boston to play all seven games before Boston was finally able to put them away. Boston showed signs of fatigue in game one, and the Cavaliers hung in there until the very end. A clutch shot by Kevin Garnett in the closing minute was enough to seal the win for Boston, 76–72.

Cleveland couldn't recover in time from the close game-one loss and got blown out in game two, 89–73. The physical play by Boston was too much for Cleveland to overcome, as LeBron was just 8 for 42 in their first two games. The series was on its way back to Cleveland, and the Cavaliers would have to find the answer quickly.

Cleveland entered game three in full desperation mode for a victory. A three-game deficit would be too much for any team to come back from, let alone against the league's best team. Cleveland was taking no chances by jumping out to an early first-quarter lead of 32–13 and never looked back. The Cavaliers steamrolled the Celtics all night en route to a 108–84 victory. LeBron and West both had 21 points each in the win. LeBron stayed hot in game four with another 21 points, and the Cavaliers pulled off the victory 88–77 to even up the series at two games apiece.

The pivotal game five of this epic series returned to the TD Garden arena in Boston. Cleveland was full of confidence and the series was up for grabs. Cleveland used a high-energy defensive effort to take a 46–43 halftime lead. The Cavaliers were shutting down the Celtics' "Big Three" and looked to have an excellent chance to steal one on the road. A familiar problem then crept up on the Cavaliers: Once again, they failed to come out ready for the second half and couldn't keep pace with the Celtics after Boston's head coach, Doc Rivers, made some key adjustments. Boston outscored the Cavaliers 29–17 in the third quarter and took a 9-point lead into the final quarter.

LeBron and the Cavaliers fought hard to make it close, but in the end Cleveland dropped game five to the Celtics, 97–89. It was a frustrating loss for the team, as they fought hard all night, but the weak third-quarter effort was their ultimate downfall. LeBron scored 35 points and West scored 21 in the losing effort. But they received almost no help at all from the bench and dropped the pivotal game.

The Cavaliers defense stepped up big-time in game six back at Cleveland by holding the Celtics to only 69 points. The Cavaliers swarmed Boston's shooters all night long and forced a deciding game seven by taking game six, 74–69. LeBron took matters into his own hands by putting up 32 points, 12 rebounds, and 6 assists. The series was headed back to Boston for a decisive game seven.

Few words in sports excite fans more than "game seven." This had been a classic series already, and the game-seven showdown was set to capture the attention of the nation. Boston had the best record in the league and was the heavy favorite to win it all; Cleveland was the defending champ with arguably the world's best player. It was the final battle of two heavyweight powers that had already gone six brutal rounds and was set for a thrilling finish.

Game seven at first looked like a blowout—Boston came out of the gate with all guns blazing. By halftime, the Celtics led 50–40 and had the Cavaliers beat in almost every category. At halftime, however, Coach Brown made some crucial adjustments that enabled the Cavaliers to come roaring back in the third quarter and cut the lead down to five points heading into the fourth quarter. Then an incredible duel between Pierce and LeBron developed, with Pierce finishing with 41 points and LeBron scoring 45. In the end, Boston did just enough to win the game 97–92 and take the series, sending Cleveland home and ending their bid to repeat as Eastern Conference Champions.

It was a hard-fought series for Cleveland in which they surprised many fans and media members with how well they played and how far they pushed Boston. It was encouraging to see the new players mesh so well together, leaving a hopeful impression that the team would only get better with a full off-season of working out and fine tuning. LeBron only had two years left on his contract, and one final push for a championship was set to begin in MVP fashion!

LeBron slaps hands with the fans on the sidelines.   Photo: Fran Morino

CHAPTER FIVE

The Ascension

The Cavaliers were on a mission to make up for their early exit in the 2008 playoffs with a dominant 2008–09 season. The task for Danny Ferry was clear: He needed to find one more piece of the puzzle for it all to fit together before another serious run at the title could be made.

A big move came on August 13, 2008, when the Cavaliers took part in a three-team trade with the Oklahoma City Thunder and the Milwaukee Bucks that saw Damon Jones and Joe Smith leave town, but in return Cleveland got sharpshooting point guard Mo Williams from the Bucks. Williams was a talented point guard who knew how to generate points with a variety of passes and smart shots. He was quick off the dribble and could create his own shot when needed. He was the perfect complement to Delonte West in the backcourt.

The Cavaliers would be tested right away. Opening night was back in Boston at the TD Garden, where Cleveland would face the defending NBA Champions once more. The Celtics picked up where they had previously left off and, despite a great effort by Cleveland, managed to put away the Cavaliers 90–85. It was clear that the Celtics would remain the team to beat.

The Cavaliers split their next two games with a win at home against the Charlotte Hornets and a loss on the road in New Orleans. It was after that loss to the Hornets that the Cavaliers caught fire and remained that way for the remainder of the season. They rolled an eight-game winning streak, highlighted by wins over the Dallas Mavericks, the Chicago Bulls, the Indiana Pacers, the Denver Nuggets, and the Utah Jazz. They had a short-lived stumbling block with a single loss to the Detroit Pistons, but they quickly bounced back with an 11-game winning streak that pushed their season record to 20–3. They lost on the road to the Atlanta Hawks before winning six more games in a row. The Cavaliers were dominating teams left and right, and by the time of the turn of the 2009 calendar year, the team held a 26–5 record. Cleveland also held a perfect home record that stood firm until the Lakers beat the Cavaliers on February 8, 2009. But even with that loss, Cleveland maintained an impressive 39–10 record and was well on the way to locking up the first overall seed.

The Cavaliers remained red-hot down the stretch with numerous winning streaks, including an impressive 13-game winning streak into late March. Perhaps most impressive of all was an April 12, 2009, win against the Boston Celtics, where the Cavaliers pounded the Celtics and won 107–76. The 31-point win was a clear statement that the Cavaliers had emerged as the new dominant team in the NBA. The Cavaliers finished with a franchise best record of 66–16. It was also the best record of any team in then-current NBA history. It also locked up home-field advantage throughout the playoffs and gave Cleveland an enormous amount of momentum heading into the playoffs.

LeBron had a season that was so good it earned him his first league MVP award. He was voted the very best player in the NBA and took home the very prestigious award. He averaged 28.4 points a game, combined with 7.6 rebounds and 7.2 assists. He was the best player on the court every night and the main reason the Cavaliers enjoyed so much success. It was nice to see the national media finally put aside their negative bias against Cleveland and grant LeBron the well-deserved award. He was, without question, the best player on the planet.

Kenny Roda gave his thoughts on why LeBron was able to have such a breakout season:

> *I think it was a combination of a number of things with LeBron James. He was able to mature a little bit more that season and was growing as an individual on and off the court. It was just his God-given abilities and understanding the game better, what teams were trying to take away from him, and what he needed to improve on. All the great ones go back and look at their game to try and add something new to it each and every off-season. Whether it's a post-up game or a better jump shot, improve your foul shots and three-pointers. Go back to Michael Jordan and Magic Johnson— they would all do that. They would all work on the things they felt their game needed to get better at in the off-season. This would help in the following seasons if teams were trying to exploit that weakness; it wasn't a weakness anymore. I think LeBron James, looking back on it now, he was wired the same way, and that is why he is going to be one of the all-time greats. The great thing about players that are that damn good, they usually want to get even better. As good as he was, he wasn't the MVP yet, and that was his motivation to step it up even more this season and win it. He wanted to be an MVP and felt that he deserved but had not yet won it—then there is that motivation. The great ones, as great as they are, always think that they can get better, and that is a great attitude to have, and LeBron has had that attitude his whole career. I think that part of the reason he broke out that season is because he felt he got slighted the year before.*

The Cavaliers opened up the playoffs against their long-time rival, the Detroit Pistons. Things were vastly different this time than just two short years earlier. The Pistons had aged, and the team was no longer the powerhouse it had once been. They were the eighth seed and seen as a heavy underdog against the highly favored Cavaliers.

The Cavaliers jumped out to a quick two-game lead in the series by dominating game one and game two at home, 102–84 and 94–82. The series headed to the Palace of Auburn Hills and the Pistons' hopes of coming back were on life support. The Cavaliers continued to roll and polished off the Pistons in Detroit by taking both games three and four, 79–68 and 99–78. Games one through three were such blowouts that by the time game four rolled around, Detroit fans didn't even bother to show up, leaving more than half of the stands full of Cleveland fans. It was such a magical season that Cleveland fans had no problem driving the 2½ hours to the Palace to support their team. It was also a vast difference from just a few years prior, when Detroit was on top of the mountain and the Cavaliers were looking to take them down at all costs.

LeBron continued to look amazing in the playoffs with efforts of 38, 29, 25, and 36 points. Despite the wide difference in win totals, LeBron knew better than to take Detroit lightly and made sure to bring his very best game to the court each night. The Cavaliers were on fire and ready to take on their second-round opponent, the Atlanta Hawks.

With such stars as Joe Johnson, Josh Smith, and Mike Bibby, the Atlanta Hawks were seen as a formidable opponent coming into the second-round series. Many broadcasters considered the Hawks good enough to push the Cavaliers to at least six, if not seven, games. Despite the talent and hype behind the Hawks, the Cavaliers didn't fear Atlanta and went right out and swept the Hawks in four games with relative ease. The Hawks couldn't compete with the high-powered

Cavalier attack. The Cavaliers averaged a 16-point victory per game. The Cavaliers had won eight straight playoff games and were looking simply unstoppable. There was nothing the Atlanta Hawks could do to even keep the games close, and head coach Mike Woodson was out of answers.

Heading into the conference semifinals, the entire league was expecting a Cleveland versus Boston rematch. The Orlando Magic had a different idea, though, and upset the Celtics in the conference semifinals. The Magic was a young and talented team, but few in the national sports media thought they would have what it would take to hang with the Cavaliers. Little did anyone know that the Cavaliers were headed for a classic series. Of the national media, only Charles Barkley had enough guts to pick against the heavily favored Cavaliers. With the way LeBron was playing, those in the media and fans alike thought it impossible for Cleveland to lose even one game on their walk to the NBA Finals and pending showdown against Kobe Bryant and the Los Angeles Lakers.

Game one against Orlando was in Cleveland, with the Cavaliers taking the homecourt advantage and jumping out to a huge lead. The Cavaliers were beating the Magic 63–48 at halftime and didn't appear to be cooling off anytime soon. Everything looked in control until the Orlando Magic came out in the third quarter and couldn't miss a shot. Orlando was suddenly on a hot shooting streak and out-scored the Cavaliers 30–19 in the third quarter. The Magic continued to remain hot throughout the rest of the game and took a 107–106 lead with only a few seconds to go. The Cavaliers were blindsided by the dramatic change of pace brought on by the Orlando Magic shooting inferno. A last-second desperation shot by Williams rattled in and out, and just like that, the Cavaliers had lost their first playoff game and were suddenly down in the series. Everyone in the NBA universe of fans and the media were stunned, as Cleveland had dominated the playoffs up until that point, and were now hoping this second-half collapse would be just a minor hiccup.

The Cavaliers had wasted a 49-point masterpiece by LeBron. The problem was that, despite his incredible scoring display, the Cavaliers' bench provided only 5 points. That was simply not acceptable and would be a major obstacle for the team to overcome if the problem continued. The best player cannot score 49 points in a losing effort— an all-around recipe for disaster for a team trying to win an NBA Championship. LeBron was playing his all-out best, but without any help from his teammates, it simply didn't matter.

Game two followed almost the exact same script as game one. The Cavaliers once again jumped out to a big lead of 30–16 after the first quarter. Sadly, just like in game one, the Magic came roaring back throughout the game until they held a 95–93 lead with only one second to go. Hedo Türkoğlu hit a clutch two-point shot to give the Magic the lead and take the wind out of the Cleveland crowd. Coach Brown drew up one last play for the Cavaliers to try and either tie the game or go for the win in the regulation. The next second in time will live forever in the great memories and moments of Cleveland sports history, as Williams inbounded the ball into the waiting hands of LeBron, who stood 25 feet away from the basketball goal. LeBron caught the ball, turned, and put up a shot that would go down easy, sending the fans of Cleveland into a frenzy of excitement! It was, at that time, the most defining moment in LeBron's career. It also summed up why he was voted league MVP that season.

The Cavaliers dropped game three in Orlando by a score of 99–89. The refereeing was horrible all night, and the Cavaliers could not stay out of foul trouble because of it. The poor officiating, combined with the Magic's hot shooting, placed Cleveland in a deep hole. The Magic suddenly had a stranglehold on the series, and the team continued to get clutch shots and not allow anyone other than LeBron to score. Williams was having a very disappointing series and wasn't providing the needed help for the Cavaliers to compete. If Williams didn't improve in a hurry and the Cleveland bench didn't wake up out of their shooting slump, the Cavaliers would be in serious trouble! Williams, quick to run his mouth as the team headed into game four, boasted an expected victory for Cleveland.

Game four in Orlando was another classic, down-to-the-wire game. Dwight Howard continued to dominate down low, causing the Cavaliers to force a double team on him and allowing Orlando open access to three-pointers. It was a double-edged sword that resulted in Cleveland getting sliced every time. Rafer Alston was able to cash in on the openings caused by the Howard double team and scored 26 points to go along with Howard's 27. Alston should not have been able to score 26 points on the North Olmsted High School JV team, let alone the Cavaliers in the playoffs!

The Cavaliers hung tough all night and, with less than a minute to go, the outcome was still in doubt. The Cavaliers led 98–97 with only 6 seconds left in the game. LeBron had just hit two clutch foul shots to give Cleveland the lead, and now the team just needed one defensive stop and the series would be tied at two. Coming out of a time-out and only down one point, it was expected that the Magic would be sure to get the ball down low to Howard for the final drive for the win. Instead, it was Türkoğlu driving the lane before kicking out to a well-covered Rashard Lewis, who hit a three-pointer with a hand in his face to give Orlando a 100–98 lead with only 4.1 seconds remaining. It was that kind of series for Orlando—everything they did seemed to go just right. It was back-breaking moment for the Cavaliers, as the team had played so well all night.

With 4.1 seconds left, the game was far from over and the Cavaliers had one last chance left to try to tie or win. Cleveland got the ball into the hands of LeBron once again, who drove the lane and was fouled putting up the shot and missed. However, because of the foul, he would have a chance to make two foul shots with only .5 seconds remaining to send the game into overtime. LeBron proved he was cold-blooded, calmly nailing both foul shots to send the game into overtime. It was a big-pressure moment handled brilliantly by the game's best player. But once again, the Cavaliers would waste an incredible effort from LeBron.

Orlando jumped out to a quick 6-point lead in overtime. Two dunks by Howard down low, combined with a three-pointer by Mickaël Piétrus had the Cavaliers in a deep hole yet again. Until that moment, most NBA fans hadn't even heard of Piétrus because he had never done anything of note prior to that point in his futile NBA career—and he never did anything of note after that moment either. LeBron kept the Cavaliers in the game by making another clutch three-pointer in addition to providing timely foul shooting. Orlando continued to use their dominant big man, Dwight Howard, down low and built a 4-point lead with only 6 seconds to go. LeBron nailed a three-pointer to cut the lead down to only one point with 3 seconds left on the clock. LeBron would not allow the Magic to put it away without giving them one hell of a fight. But after a couple of foul shots by Lewis, the Magic came ahead with the win at 116–114 and took a commanding 3–1 lead in the series.

LeBron had once again played amazingly in the loss, scoring 44 points with 12 rebounds and 7 assists. It was a familiar trend for him to play a incredible game but lack the needed support for the win. It was starting to become one of the best playoff runs by a single player in NBA history. Ilgauskas continued to have all kinds of problems with stopping Howard and couldn't play him physically enough to stop the runaway train. The weak play of Žydrūnas Ilgauskas was absolutely killing the Cavaliers' chances of winning. LeBron had been playing the best basketball of his career to this point, and the Cavaliers were still down 3–1 in the series. Things were not looking good as Cleveland returned home for game five.

Game five proved to be every bit as wild and intense as the first four. The Cavaliers once more jumped out to a huge lead in the first quarter. After one frame of play, they led 35–18. And just as in the previous games, the Cavaliers once again blew the lead and let Orlando outscore them 37–21 in the second quarter. The teams played each other close to even in the third, which set up another dramatic fourth-quarter finish.

The game was nip-and-tuck throughout the fourth quarter, until the Cavaliers finally pulled away in the end with a 112–102 victory. Down the street from the Quicken Loans Arena, popular comedian Jeff Dunham was in town for his first-ever Cleveland performance, and he had to stop several times throughout his show to give nervous fans in the crowd updates on the game. LeBron was again magnificent, pouring in 37 more points with 14 rebounds and 12 assists. It was another playoff triple-double for the reigning MVP. Williams was able to contribute as well as he chipped in with 24 points. Yet again, however, the bench was a cause for concern: Combined, they scored only 15 points.

Game six in Orlando turned out to be a disaster for the Cavaliers as the Magic jumped out to a big lead early in the game and never looked back. The one constant Orlando had was Dwight Howard flexing his muscle for big games every night—a problem for the Cavaliers in that each game had a different player stepping up big to help Howard carry the load. If the Cavaliers focused on Lewis, then Alston would step in, or whomever the special player was that evening. Cleveland simply couldn't catch a break, a fact that was evident as the Cavaliers were trailing the Magic at halftime, 58–40. The Cavaliers' dream season was ending in a nightmare.

Cleveland never scored much closer in the second half, and Orlando won game six, 103–90, clinching the series. It was a heartbreaking way for a great season to end for the Cavaliers, as they had the best record in the league and possessed the league's best player. It came as a shock to numerous pundits around the league as well. Nike was running a puppet commercial that all but directly indicated that the NBA Finals would be the Los Angeles Lakers and Kobe Bryant versus the Cleveland Cavaliers and LeBron James. No one expected Orlando, with their classic underachiever Dwight Howard and sudden group of on-point shooters, to knock off the highly touted Cleveland Cavaliers.

Kenny Roda supplied his reasoning for why the Cavaliers lost that series in upset fashion:

Matchups! Mike Brown was a big reason we lost. Mike Brown did not handle the matchups correctly. It was a series in which you had a matchup of the slower Ben Wallace on guys like Rashard Lewis, and the matchups were just awful. Mike Brown didn't match up well when the Orlando Magic elected to spread the floor and go with the perimeter. A lot of times he had LeBron guarding Alston, which meant others were being guarded by less-than-swift players and being left wide open. [Ilgauskas] matched up poorly with Dwight Howard and got picked apart all series. When you look back at that series, most of it had to do with the simple fact it was just a bad matchup series for the Cavaliers as far as the rosters and the way Mike Brown handled everything that caused them to lose. He didn't have the proper pieces maybe, but as a coach you have to adjust and find a way to win. He needed to find a way to stop their three-point shooting, and the Cavaliers were ill-equipped to do that, as the Orlando Magic were 12 of 29 in that final game. They couldn't defend the arc because of the matchup problems the Stan Van Gundy

lineup was creating for the Cavaliers. Bottom line: It was matchups
and Mike Brown that caused that loss!

What made things even more painful for the Cavaliers was that
LeBron had a truly epic series. He played out of his mind all six games,
and he almost singlehandedly beat the Orlando Magic. He averaged
an unheard-of 38.5 points, 8.3 rebounds, and 8 assists per game. It
was a shame that such an incredible effort would be wasted for a loss.
Looking strictly at the stat lines and seeing that one player on a team
had those kind of numbers, no one would have thought that the player
would have been playing for the losing team.

Jerry Mires also gave his thoughts about what went wrong in
that series:

Worst matchup possible! We were built for Boston. It was like the
Bulls and the Pistons when Jordan and the Bulls were trying to get
past the Pistons. The team in front of them was Boston, so they were
trying to put together all the pieces to beat the Celtics, and Orlando
exploited every weakness the Cavs had. That three-point shooting—I
remember [it] was lights-out. I remember working nights at my job
and watching the games on the computer and just being stunned
at how they would constantly have people wide open and everyone
was killing us. One of the games the Cavs actually won was luck
when we hit that crazy buzzer beater. I don't blame Mike Brown;
it wasn't his fault the matchups didn't work. You can have the
best game plan possible, but if the players just don't match up,
it won't work, especially against a team as good as Orlando. His
adjustments were poor at times because they moved so slowly, and
that was the one thing Mike Brown has always been bad at. But he
is great because he is patient and gives his players the benefit of the
doubt and doesn't make knee-jerk reactions. The flip side of that is,
if it doesn't work out, then people say you waited too long to make

changes. That was such a stunner because of every year of LeBron being here, that was their best shot! I would have bet my life savings that the Cavs would win the championship that year, they were that freaking good. After sweeping our way through the first two rounds, I wondered if we were even going to lose a game! The other thing was that we would be up big in the first half of each game and then throw it away in the second half. You could feel that series shifting and slipping away from the Cavs as it went. Had we gotten past them, we would have gotten past the Lakers in the NBA Finals.

The Orlando Magic went on to lose in only five games to the Los Angeles Lakers and Kobe Bryant. It was a lackluster series that had fans and media members left wondering what they could have seen with a classic Kobe Bryant versus LeBron James matchup instead. The Orlando Magic played poorly and proved they were simply a fluke team that had gotten hot at the right time.

In addition, Ken Carman gave his opinions on why the Cavaliers came up short:

Who could we defend? We just couldn't defend them! Dwight How-ard really owned us. Not a lot of people even realize that when you are so good and powerful you're hard to defend on the inside, and I'm not a Dwight Howard fan—I really don't like the guy. I thought Howard dictated that series because Mike Brown wanted to stop Howard and hoped they would get cold from the outside, but they never got cold, it just never happened. I know the game is moving away from down low and going to the wing, but this is where a dominant post player like Howard was and still can be, this is where he can truly dominate your team. You are so focused on trying to stop him that if he has good shooters around him, they are going to kill you. You are collapsing on a player who is such an offensive force that if you have another player who is on a hot night, you can just feed him the ball back out. That is what happened with Orlando the entire series. They couldn't get Rashard Lewis to miss a shot—they couldn't get anyone to miss a shot. I remember some of those games he wasn't even that good, but he was able to dictate. I just thought the Cavs caught themselves between a rock and a hard place because how are you supposed to defend Dwight Howard and then leave these hot shooters open alone beyond the arc to kill you from the three-point range. It was just a total and complete mismatch!

The Cavaliers would enter desperation mode as the off-season began. The upcoming season was the last on LeBron's contract, and the talk was fast and furious that he would be leaving town at the end of the season. If that was the case, the Cavaliers only had one more chance to win the NBA title with LeBron. No one knew what he would do, but it wasn't worth guessing, so Danny Ferry went out and traded for long-time veteran Shaquille O'Neal. Shaq was a four-time NBA Champion while playing for the Los Angeles Lakers and the Miami Heat, and many saw this as that final piece the Cavaliers needed to achieve their championship dreams. In order to obtain Shaq from the Phoenix Suns, Cleveland had to trade Wallace and Pavlović.

The move for Shaq was a desperate one, but with his pedigree, it had a high upside that outweighed the possible negatives. Shaq grew up away from his father, who possessed immense basketball talent but lived a life of trouble and stayed away from his young son. The young Shaq would spend his time at the Boys and Girls Club of America in his hometown of Newark, New Jersey, where he grew up to love the game of basketball and excel at it. He led his high school team, the Robert G. Cole Cougars, to a 68–1 record during his two years there and helped the team win the state championship during his senior year.

Shaq went on to play college basketball at Louisiana State University, where he became a two-time All-American, a two-time SEC player of the year, received the Adolph Rupp Trophy as the NCAA Men's Basketball Player of the Year in 1991, and was named the Associated Press College Basketball Player of the Year and UPI College Basketball Player of the Year. His career at LSU is one of the best in LSU basketball history, so much so that he was later inducted into the LSU Athletic Hall of Fame. Later, a 900-pound bronze statue of Shaq was erected that now stands at the entrance of the LSU Tigers Basketball Practice Facility.

By the time he left college for the NBA, it was known around the league that despite who won the draft lottery, Shaq would be the consensus number-one pick. The Orlando Magic went on to draft Shaq with the first overall pick in the 1992 NBA draft. During his rookie season, Shaq averaged 23.4 points on 56.2 percent shooting, 13.9 rebounds, and 3.5 blocks per game for the season. He was named the 1993 NBA Rookie of the Year and became the first rookie to be voted an All-Star starter since Michael Jordan in 1985. In just his first year in the NBA, Shaq became a dominant force to be reckoned with and one of the most popular athletes in all of sports! His dominance continued in year three of his career, 1994–95, when his 29.3-point average led the NBA in overall scoring. He finished second in MVP voting to David Robinson that year and was voted into his third straight All-Star game along with Hardaway.

Shaq helped Orlando to a 57–25 record in 1995 and the Atlantic Division crown. The Magic won their first-ever playoff series against the Boston Celtics and then defeated the Chicago Bulls in the conference semifinals. After beating Reggie Miller's Indiana Pacers in the 1995 Eastern Conference Championship series, the Magic reached the NBA Finals to face the defending NBA Champion, the Houston Rockets. Shaq played well in his first finals appearance, averaging

28 points on 59.5 percent shooting, 12.5 rebounds, and 6.3 assists. However, despite the incredible play of the big man in the middle, the Magic was still swept by the defending champions.

After the following season, Shaq became a free agent for the first time in his career and signed with Los Angeles amid a great deal of controversy. It was a seven-year, $121 million contract to join the Lakers, who went on to win 56 games during the 1996–97 season. Shaq averaged 26.2 points and 12.5 rebounds in his first season with Los Angeles, but he could not stay healthy all year and missed 30 games. The following season, he averaged 28.3 points and 11.4 rebounds, and he led the league with a 58.4 field-goal percentage—the first of five consecutive seasons in which he would do so. The Lakers finished the season 61–21, first in the Pacific Division, and were the second seed in the Western Conference during the 1998 NBA Playoffs. Once again, however, despite Shaq's excellent play, the Lakers fell short of the NBA Finals when they lost to the Utah Jazz, not even being able to win a single game. Shaq's plight early in his career came to be the same one LeBron would experience early in his career.

It wasn't until the Lakers made a draft-night trade for high-schooler-turned-pro shooting guard Kobe Bryant that things finally started to take shape for the team. In 2000, the Shaq–Kobe combination won the Lakers their first of three consecutive NBA Championships. Kobe and Shaq did not get along well off the court, but they still found a way to win! The Lakers beat the Indiana Pacers in 2000, the Philadelphia 76ers in 2001, and the New Jersey Nets in 2002. It was a run led by mastermind coach Phil Jackson (the same man who later would lead Michael Jordan and the Chicago Bulls to two separate three-peat runs in the 1990s). Shaq was named MVP of the NBA Finals all three of the Lakers' championship wins and had the highest scoring average for a center in NBA Finals history. Shaq was also voted the 1999–2000 regular season MVP—one vote short of becoming the first unanimous MVP in NBA history. Jackson's influence resulted in a newfound commitment by Shaq to defense, resulting in his first NBA All-Defensive Second Team selection in 2000. He also won the scoring title while finishing second in rebounds and third in blocked shots.

Continuing problems with Kobe eventually led Shaq to leave Los Angeles after the 2003–04 season. On July 14, 2004, Shaq was traded to the Miami Heat for Caron Butler, Lamar Odom, Brian Grant, and future first-round 2006 draft choice Jordan Farmar, claiming one of the main reasons he wanted to be traded to Miami was because of their up-and-coming star Dwyane Wade. In August 2005, Shaq signed a five-year-extension with the Heat for $100 million. The gamble for Shaq paid off for the Heat: The team won the NBA Championship over the Dallas Mavericks in his second year with the club.

That was the peak of his career, however—after the 2005–06 championship season, Shaq began to battle injuries. In the 2006–07 season, he missed 35 games after an injury to his left knee in November required surgery. Despite missing a large chunk of that season, Shaq reached 25,000 career points, becoming the fourteenth player in NBA history to reach that milestone. His downward spiral continued into the 2007–08 season, as he averaged career lows in points, rebounds, and blocks. His streak of 14 straight All-Star appearances ended that season, as he again missed games due to injuries, and the season was ultimately a disaster for the Heat. It was a far cry for the four-time NBA Champion. Shaq couldn't get along with head coach Pat Riley and only played in 33 games and averaged 14.2 points per game for the Miami Heat during the 2007–08 season before he was traded to the Phoenix Suns. Following the trade to Phoenix, Shaq averaged 12.9 points per game while starting all 28 games with the Suns. It was the last significant run of his career. However, at certain times, Shaq still showed flashes of his former dominant self, such as when he returned to the All-Star Game in 2009 and emerged as co-MVP along with ex-teammate Kobe Bryant. Or, later that season, when on February 27, 2009, Shaq scored 45 points and grabbed 11 rebounds, his 49th career 40-point game, beating the Toronto Raptors 133–113. The 2009 NBA Playoffs were the first time since O'Neal's rookie season in 1992–93 that he did not participate in the playoffs. He was named as a member of the All-NBA Third Team. After the trade to Cleveland, Shaq assured fans that he was going there to "win a ring for the King!"

Not everyone was excited about the acquisition of Shaq. Ken Carman had these thoughts to share: "That really wasn't Shaq—it was barely the ghost of Shaq. For the first couple of games it was just surreal to see him in a Cavs uniform, but he was falling all over the place and looking old. Looking back at it, it was a sad attempt to put something good around LeBron James."

By the All-Star break, the Cavaliers held a league-best record of 43–11. They were clicking on all cylinders again and looked to be a serious contender to return to the NBA Finals if things remained the same. However, as the team's general manger, Danny Ferry felt the Cavaliers needed one more veteran leader added to the starting lineup in time for the final playoff push. On February 17, 2010, the Cavaliers made one more trade. As part of a three-team trade, Cleveland traded Žydrūnas Ilgauskas, Emir Preldžić, and a 2010 first-round draft pick (Lazar Hayward was later selected) to the Washington Wizards; the Los Angeles Clippers traded Sebastian Telfair to the Cavaliers; the Clippers traded Al Thornton to the Wizards; the Wizards traded Antawn Jamison to the Cavaliers; and the Washington Wizards traded Drew Gooden to the Clippers. For the Cavaliers, the trade simply meant Ilgauskas for Jamison. The trade of Ilgauskas was not as shocking as it seemed, because it was well known that the Wizards would instantly cut him for salary-cap issues and he would be a free agent with the fullest intent to once again sign with the Cavaliers. In

30 days, on March 23, 2010, the Wizards did exactly that, and so the Cavaliers essentially received Antawn Jamison for nothing in return.

The Cavaliers remained hot after the trade for Jamison and the reacquisition of Ilgauskas and finished with a record of 6–21, the best overall record in the Eastern Conference once again. The Cavaliers were on a separate side of the bracket as Orlando, so many believed there would be a rematch of the prior year's classic series. The problem was that the Boston Celtics were on the same side of the bracket with Cleveland, so it forecast a possible showdown with their arch-nemesis in the second round.

LeBron was once again awarded the NBA MVP for the 2010 season. He had another stellar year, averaging 29.7 points a game with 8.6 assists and 7.3 rebounds. If this was indeed going to be his last season with Cleveland, LeBron was going out with a bang! He was now a two-time, back-to-back MVP award winner, as well as the All-Star Game MVP, leaving the last open spot on his resume for the NBA Finals MVP—and he was bound and determined that this season would fill that void.

It seemed as though everything was going according to plan as Cleveland took care of the eighth-seeded Chicago Bulls. Chicago was actually a lot better than their record that season, and they would continue to improve with future league MVP Derrick Rose leading the way. However, this series belonged to the Cavaliers, who disposed of the Bulls in five games. One special point of interest in this series was that LeBron hurt his elbow—something that would rear its ugly head in the next series games against the Boston Celtics and cause him to start taking left-handed foul shots, which remained a hotly debated subject many years later.

Boston still had their "Big Three" and were a formidable opponent for the Cavaliers in the second round. Memories were still fresh in the fans' minds of the epic seven-game series from just two years prior. Cavaliers fans hoped and prayed that this series would have a different outcome. The Cavaliers had the homecourt advantage but failed to capitalize on it, allowing Boston to split the first two games before heading to Boston for games three and four. Rumors have since spread that LeBron took the team out to celebrate his MVP award the night before game two, and that was why they all came out flat and tired and got crushed in that second game.

Game three in Boston turned into a spectacular performance by LeBron from the opening tip-off, where he put on a basketball clinic en route to a 38-point masterpiece. LeBron could have scored well over 50 points but only played 39 minutes because the Cavaliers dominated the Celtics all night long. Jamison also helped out with 20 points, and the game was never even close. Cleveland took game three by a score of 124–95, but little did anyone know that this would be the last win LeBron would ever celebrate in a Cavaliers uniform.

Everything in the NBA was about to change—and its fans were all about to play witness to it.

The wins starting occurring shortly after LeBron's arrival.   Photo: Fran Morino

CHAPTER SIX

Taking His Talents to South Beach

Lebron began to feel the pressure of the expiring contract well before game four in the Boston Celtics series. He had heard it from the fans and media for the past three years, and everyone wanted to know if he would stay in Cleveland when the contract was up. The bigger question, however, was would he take Cleveland to their long-awaited championship win before decision time came to stay or to go? So much pressure and so many questions were on the line as the Boston series intensified. Up until this point the organization and LeBron had done a great job of ignoring the questions and the pressure about his possible departure. The focal point always remained the same: to win a championship. All that would change, though, heading into game five.

The Cavaliers had dropped game four of the series a few days earlier, which brought the series back to Cleveland tied at two games apiece. There was a slight chance that if the Cavaliers failed to win, it could be the last time LeBron would ever play at home in front of Cleveland fans as a member of the Cavaliers. Many people dismissed the chance of that actually happening, but for the first time ever, it seemed that immense pressure had finally gotten to LeBron.

Things started off smoothly, with the Cavaliers leading at the end of the first quarter, 23–20. It was in the second quarter that things started to go horribly wrong: Boston outscored the Cavaliers 30–21 and never looked back from there, as the Cavaliers simply went into self-destruct mode. All five starters from Boston scored in the double digits, including Glen Davis, coming off the bench to score 15. The Cavaliers defensive effort was terrible, and they seemed to sleepwalk through the final three quarters of the game. By the time the game ended, the Cavaliers were on the losing end of a 120–88 blowout. The fans in attendance were shocked by the poor play of their team in such a crucial game. Even worse was the subpar effort of their best player. Everyone was left wondering what had gone wrong.

It would forever be remembered by Cleveland fans as the "Game Five Debacle," or, in not-so-flattering terms, "the night that LeBron choked." LeBron, who was one of the best playoff players in the NBA for several years, had his worst game in his playoff career. He seemed slow and uncaring the entire night. He wasn't his normally aggressive self and passed off many shots instead of driving to the hole. He finished with only 15 points, shooting a meager 20 percent on 14 shots, and he was also low on attempts. It was, without question, his worst overall night as a pro. He simply didn't seem to care and played without his best effort, leaving the task of winning up to his teammates. Shaq did his best to try and help out with 21 points, but it wasn't nearly enough. Rumors exploded almost immediately following the game that a pregame locker-room scuffle had thrown the team off balance.

People turned very hard on LeBron following this awful night, and Ken Carman provided his thoughts on why this occurred:

I very much think that LeBron pouted in that game. He became frustrated and let the game get the best of him instead of stepping up and becoming the best player on the court. This is another case of when the regular season can be a cruel mystery because the Celtics were far better than their number four seed, and the Cavaliers got fat off of cream puff teams such as the Charlotte Bobcats. They won 61 games and you get to the postseason and you have to actually play good teams. Once you go to a series against a good team that you have to play each night, it becomes much different. You have to figure out a new way to beat your opponent each night. It is very tough to do, as opposed to the regular season. I think that the regular season can be such a huge thing for so many people, but I believe that it can be such a mystery for so many reasons. Once you get to the postseason in the NBA, guys start playing defense and guys rise to the occasion. Even guys who haven't played much all year decide to step it up. Look at Paul Pierce of Boston as a perfect example. He may not do anything for you in the regular season, but he is there to make his money by coming up huge in the postseason. Those older players, the coaches are just trying to keep them around, get them their minutes, and get them ready for the postseason. The players are fine with it because they know they are supposed to shine in the postseason—guys like Ray Allen, for example, are the same way. I think when you get to that level, you find out who the real teams are in the postseason. We just got our hopes up so high during the regular season. Once you get to the playoffs, it becomes a completely different game. For LeBron, the frustration and pouting took over for him along with the "whatever" elbow injury. When he took his jersey off, it was like watching a frustrated child walking off that floor. Years later, he learned how to lose like a man, but at that time he was just an angry kid. It was like hanging up the phone on your girlfriend and not wanting to talk to her the rest of the night. In this case, he hung up on us and didn't want to talk with us for four years.

Jerry Mires also gave his thoughts on what occurred at the end of that series:

> *You cannot convince me that LeBron James did not quit! You can-not convince me that the series wasn't as close to fraud that has ever been committed in the NBA. That team was still a talented team. Guys like Antawn Jamison were picked up, and he is still good years later. LeBron had a piece at bringing players in. He had conversa-tions and helped make the roster choices. The clock that he put the Cavs in was no helping matter either. They were in win-now mode, and he pouted.*

Considering LeBron's total body of work, the opposite argument could be made that he did not choke and simply had an off game. If it weren't for LeBron, Cleveland wouldn't have gotten as far as the team did. The guy had one bad night—that doesn't erase seven prior years straight of great nights! If it weren't for him in the Orlando series the year before, Cleveland would have been swept and lost each game by at least 30 points. The fact that people still crucify the man for one bad game is insane! Referees in basketball can fix a game—as can be demonstrated to happen—but this was not LeBron throwing a game. Something was clearly wrong in his head that night, and he let it get the best of him. The fact that anyone would even think he would throw the game because he knew he was leaving is a major point of contention.

With the misery of game five still fresh, the Cavaliers headed back to Boston for game six, clinging to hope that LeBron would reemerge and force a game seven. LeBron answered his heavy critics from game five and responded with a great effort, scoring 27 points with 19 rebounds and 10 assists. It was another incredible playoff triple-double performance from LeBron, but it was too little too late and the Celtics were simply unstoppable. Boston ended Cleveland's playoff run by a score of 94–85.

Roda shared his thoughts on what went wrong in that final series game against Boston:

I wish I knew why he did what he did in game five. Some people say that he choked, others feel that he didn't choke, he just pouted. He had seven turnovers, and it killed him because Boston knew how to defend him. They tilted the floor and, when Anthony Parker and Mo Williams are your other options, you're in trouble. If you're Boston, you let those guys try and beat you and focus your coverage on LeBron James. Maybe the pressure got to him. Some people said that he had severe anxiety on the level of almost having panic attacks. The weight of the world was on his shoulders, and he was unable to handle that, or he was simply fed up without getting any help. He was carrying so much. Before game two, when he got his MVP trophy, there was talk that he had the guys out late celebrating. That's why they got their doors blown off in game two of that series. I don't know if they let up or what the deal was in that series, but it is still a mystery to me what happened after going up two games to one in that series. There are theories that he choked under the pressure, other theories that he already had his sights set on Miami. All kinds of excuses and theories, and I don't know which one is right. It could be a combination of all of them. He choked, they let up after being up, and his mind was elsewhere—no one truly knows but LeBron James.

For the second straight year, the Cavaliers had the best record in the Eastern Conference. For the second straight year, they had the league's MVP. And, sadly, for the second straight year, they failed to reach the NBA Finals. It was clear that the specter of LeBron's possible departure from Cleveland made for too much of a distraction. In the end, it may have been their biggest downfall, and now they had to anguish through the rest of the postseason at home, as well as the early part of the off-season, wondering and waiting to see if LeBron would resign from the team.

LeBron did not take the normal route of free agency, in which players meet with several teams on the side and eventually make a decision on where they'll go next. Most times a tweet is sent out by the agent or team calling for a press conference, and then an official announcement is made. Instead of taking the normal, low-key, humble way of doing things, LeBron was talked into having a media circus by LRMR, the management group that handled all of his media appearances and business deals. There were several big-name free agents available that off-season, and LeBron called a summit in order to allow them all to talk things over. Such a move was previously unheard of—having numerous players come together and discuss what their plans were for free agency. It reeked of collusion and was only about to get worse.

The 2010 free agency class was loaded with NBA superstars, including LeBron James, Dwyane Wade, Chris Bosh, Amar'e Stoudemire, Dirk Nowitzki, Carlos Boozer, and Joe Johnson. Where these players would eventually decide to go would greatly reshape the entire NBA for a long time to come.

While the free-agent madness was under way, the Cavaliers front office was in a state of great transition. On June 4, 2010, Danny Ferry left the Cavaliers with one month left on his contract. The Cavaliers went 272–138 during his reign as general manager. Head coach Mike Brown had also been fired a few weeks prior on May 24, 2010.

The Cavaliers were attempting to clean house in the hopes that LeBron would stay if they brought in a high-profile coach and general manager. Cleveland ended up having Chris Grant, former vice president of the Atlanta Hawks who came to work with the

Cavaliers under Ferry in 2005, take over as general manager—a decision that turned out to be a large failure over the course of the next several years.

The search for a new head coach took a little longer than expected, as Cleveland failed in an attempt to acquire legendary college head coach Tom Izzo, whom they had hoped to lure away from Michigan State University. Izzo would choose to remain in the college ranks, and Cleveland's search for a head coach would have to continue elsewhere.

On July 2, 2010, Byron Scott was named head coach of the Cleveland Cavaliers. He had an extremely successful career while playing in Los Angeles as a member of the "Showtime" Lakers. He was a starter alongside Magic Johnson, James Worthy, Kareem Abdul-Jabbar, and A. C. Green, and he had played for the Lakers for 10 consecutive seasons, from 1983 to 1993. During that time he was also on three NBA Championship teams in 1985, 1987, and 1988. In short, Scott came with a championship pedigree.

When his playing career ended, Scott took over the coaching reins for the New Jersey Nets in 2000. The team initially struggled that first season, but then caught fire and won 52 games the following season. The Nets reached the NBA Finals before losing to Scott's former team, the Los Angeles Lakers. He led the Nets right back to the championship round the following season as well, this time losing to the San Antonio Spurs. Despite the back-to-back finals' losses, it was still seen as a huge turnaround for the Nets in a very short amount of time. Scott was seen as one of the best coaches in the NBA, which was why it came as shock the following season when he was fired from New Jersey after a 22–20 start. It was a bizarre move by the Nets upper management that sent shock waves throughout the NBA, though once reports of Scott's off-the-court demeanor started to trickle in, the move no longer seemed controversial.

Scott would then catch on as head coach of the New Orleans Hornets the following year in an attempt to reclaim his championship ways. Things did not go well at the outset of Scott's tenure with the Hornets; the team missed the playoffs his first three seasons there. Entering the 2007–08 season, the Hornets finally turned it around with star point guard Chris Paul and finished first in the NBA Western Conference Southwest Division. The Hornets made it to the Conference Semifinals before losing to the San Antonio Spurs. The Hornets were having their best season since coming to New Orleans, so it came as another shock when, nine games into the 2009–10 season, Scott was fired again.

The Cavaliers liked what Scott had shown he could do with all-star players and young superstars in the past, and they hoped that he would be the perfect coach to convince LeBron to remain in town. One by one, the other free agents were making their decisions. Nowitzki decided to stay in Dallas and re-sign with the Mavericks. Bosh left Toronto to play for the Miami Heat, where Wade had just re-signed. Boozer neglected to come back to Cleveland, and instead signed with the Chicago Bulls. Stoudemire elected to leave Phoenix for the New York Knicks. Things were taking shape, and LeBron was the last big name remaining to sign with a team.

All that would change on July 10, 2010, when LeBron put on one of the biggest media spectacles ever seen. Instead of signing a contract and making an announcement with his agent, he decided it would be best to go on national television with infamous sportscaster Jim Gray. The broadcast was from the Boys and Girls Club of Greenwich, Connecticut, and ultimately raised $2.5 million for the charity and an additional $3.5 million in advertising revenue that was donated to various other charities. ESPN was in charge of airing the media circus and scheduled it for primetime. The program started at 9 p.m., but it wasn't until 28 minutes into the show that LeBron finally announced his decision to join fellow All-Stars Bosh and Wade to play for the Miami Heat. His exact words were as follows:

In this fall . . . this is very tough . . . in this fall I'm going to take my talents to South Beach and join the Miami Heat. I feel like it's going to give me the best opportunity to win and to win for multiple years, and not only just to win in the regular season or just to win five games in a row or three games in a row, I want to be able to win championships. And I feel like I can compete down there.

Carman provided his insight as to why LeBron chose this format to make such a horrible announcement and embarrass Cleveland:

I really do think that it happened for a multitude of reasons. First and foremost, there was a lot of bad information with the people around him that completely ruined his image for a year or two. It didn't ruin his skills on the court but his perception amongst fans. He was able to rebuild his rep, but during that time he completely mishandled that. His company LRMR really didn't know how to handle something like that. They were his buddies, and they should have done it in a much better fashion than in the way they did it on national television. Earlier in the day, reporters were saying he was leaving for Miami and it was a done deal. I thought to myself, "No way. He is going on national television; there is no way he is leaving." Guys get this stuff wrong all the time—hell, look at Rick Bucher, who reported he was staying in Cleveland that morning. So when he goes on television, it was just such a surreal moment and I thought to myself, "My God!" People thought we would still win 40 games without him, and that did not happen. At that time it was just such a poor decision, as I think he was in cahoots with his buddies. He loves Bosh and Dwyane Wade, although I cannot stand Dwyane Wade as I feel he has become such a child during the last few years. I feel Bosh has gotten better and someone I really respect as far as a basketball player and a person—same with LeBron. I just think that Wade has kind of morphed into this childish mentality and taking cheap shots at other players. Because I think Wade is struggling with the fact that he is losing steps day-by-day and is only 32. Father Time has been cruel to him and robbed him of his skills. He has just been taking cheap shots and acting very childish. He was supposed to be a leader and instead he became a Jimmy Hart/Mouth of the South–type of person, as his bark became bigger than his bite. He is out there doing cough jokes about Dirk when he was sick, he was telling people to call him "three," he's wearing Capri pants and it's just not a good look for him. Meanwhile, you have Chris Bosh, and people can make their jokes about dinosaurs and other various remarks, but he is intelligent and a good husband and teammate. He really is someone I have come to respect as a fan. If you analyze it even as a fan, even after he has killed a lot of fans with kindness, James saw a chance to play with his buddies and didn't realize the backlash coming against him. He had people put it in his head that we were LeBron fans and not Cavs fans. When he made that decision and then saw the immediate hateful backlash of jerseys being burned and everything else, he was sincerely surprised. He was legitimately shocked by it, and I think that has stuck with him the whole time. His family was very upset by it, and that bugged him. I understand where his family is coming from because that is their son, brother, husband, and father—that is a big deal. You want your family and friends to like you and do right by them. It makes it tough for a guy like that who is from here and needed that connection. There are a lot of good friends and family here in Ohio, even for athletes after they leave. It will give them the draw of coming home.

The television program drew high ratings, and Nielsen reported that an average of 9.9 million people watched the show in the United

States, with 13.1 million tuning in at the time of LeBron's announcement. Not surprisingly, Cleveland topped all markets with a 26 Nielsen rating and a 39 share. The show's Nielsen ratings were 6.1 in households and 4.1 in 18–49, making it the most watched cable show of the night.

Kenny Roda offered valuable insight into the debacle on ESPN that evening:

The worst night in Cleveland sports history for me covering Cleveland sports. I'm a basketball guy first. For me, thinking he was returning, then he goes on national television to announce that he wasn't returning and to rip the hearts out of Cavaliers fans and Clevelanders, it was devastating to me as a fan, Cavs fans everywhere, the team, and the city both emotionally and financially with him leaving. It was just one of those nights that you will never forget where you were and what you were doing. No one could believe that it happened and now, years later, he is able to admit it was a mistake as to how it all went down. He wishes he could go back and do it a different way. It was just a devastating night for everyone involved. The effect that it had on me as a parent—my son had just graduated from high school and was crushed by the news—it had a terrible effect on him, and when someone harms your child in any way, shape or form, you're not very fond of that person. With the way LeBron James made the announcement, he harmed my child because he upset him, and an upset child is not something as a parent that you feel good about because you can't do anything to control it. So it is a day that I will never forget. But with everything that has happened now, looking back on it now, he was just immature in how he handled it.

One particular comment of LeBron's during his announcement sparked instant criticism: Instead of being humble, he talked about his "talents" and referred to Miami as "South Beach." That one remark displayed appalling immaturity and selfishness. He didn't need to stay in Cleveland because he had every legal right to leave, but it was how he went about it that upset everyone watching—one does not go on national television and embarrass one's hometown the way he did. The gaffe not only set Cleveland fans ablaze, it quickly made LeBron James one of the most hated men in sports.

Jerry Mires also weighed in on the debacle:

Those guys knew what they were doing years earlier, and it was total collusion. That's why they signed contracts that would expire in the same year. They knew as far back as 2008, when they were playing in the Olympics, what they were planning on doing. They put this whole plot together back then. Once LeBron made up his mind, it was all over. He threw the series because he knew if they went further then he couldn't leave, and that is why he pulled that crap with his elbow that you have never heard about again! Forget the stupid TV spectacle—people should be pissed because he faked an elbow injury and threw the series. He's supposed to be a freak of nature and the best athlete in sports, and yet he is screwing around with left-handed free throws. That pissed me off! Look at some of the mistakes he made— you can't tell me that he wasn't throwing it. He was kicking balls out of bounds. He was doing things that he has never done in his life. I'm not talking about making mistakes, because everyone makes mistakes. He was making intentional *mistakes! Mike Brown is up yelling, and LeBron tells him to sit down. When he storms off that court and rips off his jersey, I don't know why anyone in Cleveland thought he was coming back. How could any of us have been surprised? That thing was orchestrated! If the Cavs would have won, it would have hurt the next phase of his career.*

Cleveland fans instantly revolted against LeBron and could be seen burning replicas of his jersey in the streets. LeBron was later quoted as saying that the whole ordeal may have been a mistake on his part, but that he stood by his decision. On September 29, 2010, when asked by Soledad O'Brien of CNN if race was a factor in the fallout from his decision, LeBron replied, "I think so, at times. There's always, you know, a race factor." It was mind-blowing to many that LeBron would use this rationale to explain why fans were so mad at him. Race had nothing to do with it, however: The only color Cavaliers fans saw was red—as in anger.

LeBron's move to join two fellow All-Stars in Miami was also criticized by former greats of the NBA. This had never been done before, and it had everyone in an uproar. Michael Jordan stated that he would not have contacted his rivals from other teams like Magic Johnson and Larry Bird to play on one team together. Jordan stated, "I wanted to defeat those guys," adding, "Things are different now. I can't say that's a bad thing. It's an opportunity these kids have today."

Neither LeBron nor his agents had the courtesy to contact anyone at the Cleveland Cavaliers organization to notify them of their decision before the televised announcement. Owner Dan Gilbert did not hesitate to vent his frustration at the situation, and he tried to comfort the fans with a solid vote of confidence in the Cavaliers' ability as a team without LeBron.

Gilbert penned the following letter, which was posted on social media in a matter of minutes following the decision:

Dear Cleveland, all of Northeast Ohio, and Cleveland Cavaliers supporters wherever you may be tonight:

As you now know, our former hero, who grew up in the very region that he deserted this evening, is no longer a Cleveland Cavalier.

This was announced with a several day, narcissistic, self-promotional build-up culminating with a national TV special of his "decision" unlike anything ever "witnessed" in the history of sports and probably the history of entertainment.

Clearly, this is bitterly disappointing to all of us.

The good news is that the ownership team and the rest of the hard-working, loyal, and driven staff over here at your hometown Cavaliers have not betrayed you nor NEVER will betray you.

There is so much more to tell you about the events of the recent past and our more than exciting future. Over the next several days and weeks, we will be communicating much of that to you.

You simply don't deserve this kind of cowardly betrayal.

You have given so much and deserve so much more.

In the meantime, I want to make one statement to you tonight:

"I PERSONALLY GUARANTEE THAT THE CLEVELAND CAVALIERS WILL WIN AN NBA CHAMPIONSHIP BEFORE THE SELF-TITLED FORMER 'KING' WINS ONE."

You can take it to the bank.

If you thought we were motivated before tonight to bring the hardware to Cleveland, I can tell you that this shameful display of selfishness and betrayal by one of our very own has shifted our "motivation" to previously unknown and previously never experienced levels.

Some people think they should go to heaven but NOT have to die to get there.

Sorry, but that's simply not how it works.

This shocking act of disloyalty from our homegrown "chosen one" sends the exact opposite lesson of what we would want our children to learn. And "who" we would want them to grow up to become.

But the good news is that this heartless and callous action can only serve as the antidote to the so-called "curse" on Cleveland, Ohio.

The self-declared former "King" will be taking the "curse" with him down South. And until he does "right" by Cleveland and Ohio, James (and the town where he plays) will unfortunately own this dreaded spell and bad karma.

Just watch.

Sleep well, Cleveland.

Tomorrow is a new and much brighter day. . . .

I PROMISE you that our energy, focus, capital, knowledge and experience will be directed at one thing and one thing only: DELIVERING YOU the championship you have long deserved and is long overdue. . . .

Dan Gilbert

Majority Owner

Cleveland Cavaliers

It was comforting to Cleveland fans that the owner of the team would show such confidence in the team and city. He showed that he was willing to stick up for Cleveland and its die-hard fans. The city was in pain, and with local sports talk host Aaron Goldhammer constantly putting the city down and laughing at Cleveland, it was nice to see a man with the power of Gilbert fight on behalf of the city.

Carman was also upset with LeBron leaving, but he did point out the following:

The only good part I can think of is after he left—after my frustration and anger went away—I could kind of sit back and watch him and marvel at what he actually does and what his teams have been able to do. He allowed teams to work as a symphony on the offensive end and how good they were on the defensive end as well. I started to find an appreciation for his overall game, but I think that some people, when they see that incredible talent, they take athletes for granted, especially in a game like basketball. Not so much football because it's such a team sport. And it's not like that in baseball, because you're going to get four chances a day at the plate and may just get a couple of balls hit to you. But basketball is really that sport [where] you can take overwhelming talent for granted.

Mary Schmitt Boyer, former Cavaliers beat reporter for *The Plain Dealer,* also offered her opinion on how the entire spectacle was handled:

He had the right to do what he did, but the way he handled it was incorrect. I think if he had it to do over again, I don't think he would have handled it the way he did. He was young, and I don't know if he got bad advice or what his reasoning was. It could have been handled in a much better way. He could have said that he had given Cleveland what he could for seven years and it was time, but he didn't. I just think there was a way to exit with far less fanfare. Part of me thinks that he had never been away from home, as opposed to kids who go away for college, and I think at that age that maybe he felt it was time to try something else. I don't think he had animosity towards the city of Cleveland, I just think he thought it was time to try something else. He had given Cleveland seven marvelous years and lit the city up like Vegas, just like he promised he would. I know there are still people who will never forgive him for what he did. He could have done it in a different way.

This same sentiment remains with most who "witnessed" the decision: that LeBron had every right to leave, but the way he chose to do it hurt many Clevelanders. It's like anything else in life—no one wants to see a loved one or a loved team leave town, but it is how they depart that can speak volumes in how you heal from the loss. The departure of LeBron and how he went about it created a large wound that may never quite heal in the hearts of many war-torn Cleveland fans.

LeBron James quickly became the face of Cleveland sports. Photo: kennyroda.com

CHAPTER SEVEN

"Not One"

From the first second LeBron left Cleveland for Miami, it was seen as a sure thing by the national media and the majority of fans that the Heat would win several titles in a row right away. Miami's "Big Three" made no bones about it—the very next night after LeBron's announcement, he, Wade, and Bosh appeared wearing their new uniforms in front of an assembly arena of Miami Heat fans for a public rally. During the rally, LeBron grabbed the microphone and bragged that the team would win not one but up to seven championships in a row. It was a bold statement to make—one that he would be mocked for quickly after.

LeBron was right to be cocky, considering the talent he was joining. The combination of the trio's skills was an assembly of talent only seen on all-star teams of the past. As a child growing up in Chicago, Wade idolized Chicago Bulls' star Michael Jordan and did his best to pattern his game after his superstar hero. In his senior year of high school at Harold L. Richards High School in Oak Lawn, Wade averaged 27 points and 11 rebounds per game while leading his team to a 24–5 record. During this time, he also set the school's records for points (676) and steals (106) in a season. Despite his success in high school, Wade was recruited by only three college basketball teams due to academic problems—forming a proverbial chip on his shoulder.

The first season Wade was eligible to play with Marquette University was a strong one. He led the Golden Eagles in scoring with 17.8 points per game, led the conference in steals at 2.47 per game, and accumulated averages of 6.6 rebounds and 3.4 assists per game. The following season, 2002–03, Wade led the team again in scoring with 21.5 points per game, and they won their first and only Conference USA Championship title with a 27–6 record. Wade led the Golden Eagles to a Final Four appearance and was named to the All-America First Team by the Associated Press and as the Midwest Regional MVP. His career at Marquette was so great that the university retired his jersey in 2007 at the halftime show during a game that year.

Wade was selected fifth by the Miami Heat in the star-studded, talent-packed 2003 NBA draft, the same draft year that also featured LeBron James, Chris Bosh, and Carmelo Anthony. His rookie season went well: He averaged 16.2 points on 46.5 percent shooting, with averages of 4 rebounds and 4.5 assists per game. Wade earned a unanimous selection to the 2004 NBA All-Rookie Team and was ranked in the top five among rookies in several major statistical categories, including second in field-goal percentage, second in steals, third in scoring, fourth in assists, and fourth in minutes played.

His second year in the league was highlighted by the addition of three-time NBA Champion Shaquille O'Neal. The addition of Shaq helped Wade improve his game, and the team reached the 2005 NBA Eastern Conference Championship series where they lost to the Detroit Pistons. By the 2005–06 season, Wade had developed into one of the most prominent players in the NBA and was elected to his second All-Star Game (where he started next to future teammate LeBron James). Aided by Shaq, the 2005–06 season was another stellar one for Wade, as he averaged 27.2 points, 6.7 assists, 5.7 rebounds, and 1.95 steals per game.

The Heat remained hot that season and reached the 2006 NBA Finals where they took on the Dallas Mavericks. The Heat fell behind 2–0 in the series before Wade took matters into his own hands. His performance in games three, four, and five—in which he scored 42, 36, and 43 points, respectively—resulted in three straight wins and gave his team new life in the series. The Heat went on to win game six behind Wade's 36 points, winning the series 4–2. In only his third year in the league, Wade was awarded the Finals MVP Trophy while LeBron watched it all unfold from home in Cleveland (the Cavaliers had been knocked out of the playoffs in the second round).

The next few seasons for Wade and the Heat did not go so well, with the team plagued by injuries. Wade was never quite the same as he was in that magical third season, though he had high hopes that his two new teammates, LeBron James and Chris Bosh, would bring back the glory days and championship gold he had enjoyed early in his career.

Chris Bosh had experienced plenty of high moments in his young career already, dating back to his days playing for Lincoln High School in Dallas. While there, he won several awards, including being named High School Player of the Year by Basketball America. He was also voted Powerade Player of the Year in Texas; a First Team All-American by *Parade*, McDonald's, and EA Sports; a Second Team All-American by *USA Today* and *SLAM* magazine; a First Team All-State player; and as "Mr. Basketball" in Texas by the Texas Association of Basketball Coaches.

Bosh attended college at Georgia Tech and, in his one and only season there (2002–03), led the Yellow Jackets in averaging 15.6 points, 9 rebounds, and 2.2 blocks in 31 games and led the Atlantic Coast Conference in field goal percentage. He was selected fourth overall by the Toronto Raptors in the 2003 NBA draft. His seven years in Toronto were solid, and he became known as one of the best big men in the game. By the time he was a free agent, he was the most coveted "big man" free agent in the class.

The Miami Heat had their three superstars, but they still needed to fill out the roster around them. Seeking out veteran talent, they signed sharp shooter Mike Miller, who had played on several teams since coming into the league in 2001 with the Orlando Magic. He was known for his ability to hit three-pointers and clutch shots when called upon. LeBron was also able to talk his good friend and Cavaliers legend Žydrūnas Ilgauskas into leaving Cleveland and coming to Miami in free agency. It was another fatal blow for Cleveland.

The Heat weren't done building their dream team yet, though. Veteran power forward Juwan Howard was signed next. A former member of the famed "Fab Five" at the University of Michigan a decade earlier, Howard was a veteran leader who would be able to add a presence down low and bring leadership stability to the locker room. Up next on Pat Riley's free-agent shopping spree was Eddie House. He had been a hot prospect out of Arizona State University, and he had played for the Heat before (2000–03), but he had yet to reach his massive potential in the pros and subsequently bounced around from team to team over the years. Re-signing House to the Heat seemed to be a perfect fit for his skill set in 2010. Miami finished their shopping spree by signing Erick Dampier—a center with vast experience who could battle for rebounds and score down low.

The coach charged with leading this sudden dream team to victory was third-year man Erik Spoelstra. He had led them to 43 and 47 wins in his first two seasons as head coach; however, both seasons ended in the first round of the playoffs. Many believed that Riley would replace Spoelstra as head coach if things didn't get off to the strong start that was expected.

As a star basketball player at Jesuit High School in Beaverton, Oregon, Spoelstra, who had several college scholarship offers, chose to stay in his hometown and play for the University of Portland. His college career got off to a great start: In 1989, he was named West Coast Conference Freshman of the Year. He proved his leadership ability as the Pilots' starting point guard for four years, averaging 9.2 points, 4.4 assists, and 2.4 rebounds per game. His career at UP was so impressive that he is a member of the school's 1,000-point club and is among the Pilots' career leaders in several statistical categories. He had basketball in his blood—his father, Jon Spoelstra, was a former NBA executive of the Buffalo Braves, the Portland Trail Blazers, the Denver Nuggets, and the New Jersey Nets, but he also demonstrated that he had a mind to go along with his athletics when he graduated from UP in 1992 with a degree in communications.

Spoelstra decided not to follow his degree but instead pursue a future with his first love of basketball. Upon graduating from UP, he was hired and spent two years as a player and assistant coach for TuS Herten, a professional-basketball club based in Westphalia, Germany. It was during this time that Spoelstra took his first head-coaching job with a local youth club team. In 1995, Spoelstra was offered another two-year contract with the club, but the Miami Heat also offered him a position. It was a no-brainer for Spoelstra, and he left for the NBA.

Spoelstra was hired as the Heat's video coordinator, and it was the perfect chance for him to get his foot in the door while learning from coaching legend Pat Riley. He showed his great work ethic and commitment to the team and, after two years as video coordinator, went on to serve two years as an assistant coach. Spoelstra was then promoted to assistant coach and advance scout in 1999, and he later became the Heat's assistant coach and director of scouting in 2001. He was a man of many titles and talents, and it was clear that the

Miami Heat brain trust predicted big things for his future to have given him so many roles with the team.

Serving under Pat Riley, Spoelstra helped develop the young phenom Dwyane Wade and was given credit in helping Wade with his shot and overall game. While serving under Riley in 2006, Spoelstra was a key component in the coaching staff that won an NBA Championship that year with a six-game series victory over the Dallas Mavericks.

After the 2008 season came to an end, Spoelstra was offered the vacant head-coaching job after Pat Riley stepped down from the bench to focus solely on his role in the front office. It was Spoelstra's opportunity to prove that his long journey and work ethic could pay off on the highest level. He came in with high opinion from Riley, who was quoted as saying, "This game is now about younger coaches who are technologically skilled, innovative, and bring fresh new ideas. That's what we feel we are getting with Erik Spoelstra. He's a man that was born to coach." The faith of Pat Riley in his new coach would prove to be vital in the coming years. Spoelstra was also a trailblazer, becoming the first-ever Asian American NBA head coach as well as the first-ever Asian American head coach in the history of the four major North American sports leagues.

Spoelstra faced a tall task in taking over a team that had the league's worst record the year before: 15–67. Now, with the added superstars, the pressure would be immense on Spoelstra to win multiple NBA Championships, as anything less would not be tolerated by the fans or media. Miami fans could be very fickle, as they had a history of not supporting their teams even in good times—they would rarely sell out their arenas and stadiums even for the biggest of games. If the Heat were losing in the fourth quarter, instead of cheering louder and trying to inspire their team to make a comeback, their fans were known to simply get up and leave. Miami fans didn't have one tenth of the loyalty and passion that fans from Cleveland possessed.

However, the opening night of the Celtics versus the Miami Heat with LeBron, Wade, and Bosh had the stadium filled. The game was nationally televised, and the ratings were extremely high—many sports fans in general wanted to see just how dynamic this incredible dream team would be. The game was the most-watched NBA contest ever on cable television, earning a 4.6 rating and delivering to 7.4 million total viewers and 5.3 million households.

The game itself, however, was not the coming-out party for a Miami dynasty, because the expected offensive explosion never happened. The stingy Boston defense held the high-powered Miami attack to only 80 total points, and the Heat lost, 88–80. LeBron did his part with an impressive showing of 31 points, 3 assists, and 4 rebounds. The problem was a familiar one for LeBron: His supporting cast failed to show up. Wade was held to 13 points and scored only 8. As for the other two starters, Carlos Arroyo scored only 3 points, and Joel Anthony had just 2. No one coming off the bench that night was able to score in double digits.

The Miami Heat bounced back from the disappointing opening-night loss with a four-game winning streak, beating the Philadelphia 76ers, the Orlando Magic, the New Jersey Nets, and the Minnesota Timberwolves by double-digit margins. The team was 4–1 before things again took a wrong turn, and the Heat went on to lose 8 of their next 13 games, lowering their record to a mediocre 9–8. Many in the media didn't have them losing 8 games all season, let alone in the first month.

This slow start was attributed to many factors, one of which was the lack of cohesiveness. The team also suffered from injuries to key role players Mike Miller and Udonis Haslem. The team called a players-only meeting with the intention of encouraging the players to communicate better with each other. It was widely rumored that Spoelstra could lose his job and that Pat Riley would return as head coach. There had already been a well-publicized incident when LeBron "bumped" into Spoelstra during a time-out. The Heat rebounded through this time, however, and got things back on track with a 12-game winning streak, of which 10 came by double-digit margins as the team was finally beginning to hit their full stride. The Heat also played great defense during that stretch, limiting their opponents to fewer than 100 points each game.

LeBron returned to Cleveland on December 2, 2010, to face the Cleveland Cavaliers in front of a hostile crowd. It didn't faze the Chosen One, however, and he led the Heat to defeat his former team by scoring 38 points, dishing out 8 assists, and pulling down 5 rebounds. In the process, he tied a Heat record for points scored in a quarter with 24 points in the third. The crowd was irate all game long, and it proved to be one of the most violent crowd reactions in the history of professional sports—several fights broke out during the course of the game as LeBron exploded in scoring and the Cavaliers started to get crushed. The game drew nearly 7.1 million television viewers and earned a 25.4 rating in Miami.

The Heat was red-hot, setting a franchise record of 15 wins that December and also setting an NBA record for consecutive on-the-road victories of 10 wins in a calendar month. The game on Christmas Day wasn't even close: The Heat crushed two-time defending NBA Champions the Los Angeles Lakers. The Heat was rolling along and racking up the victories.

LeBron's popularity didn't seem to take a hit around the rest of the league, as he was once again voted to start in the All-Star Game. His teammates Wade and Bosh would be joining him, Wade in the starting lineup and Bosh as a reserve off the bench. Despite all the bitterness hanging in the air in Cleveland, the popularity of the "Big Three" didn't seem to be hurting LeBron anywhere else.

The Heat finished the regular season with a 58–24 record, good enough for the second-best record in the Eastern Conference and behind only the Chicago Bulls and league MVP Derrick Rose. It was an impressive season, but it didn't come without some drama and very rough patches. The Heat lost the season series to the defending Eastern Conference champion the Boston Celtics, 3–1; was swept by the Chicago Bulls, 3–0; and also lost both times to the Dallas Mavericks. The team also hit a dry spell after the All-Star break when, on March 3, 2011, the Heat was leading the Magic by 24 points in the third quarter before being outscored 40–9, losing 99–96. The following night against the Spurs, who held the NBA's best record (51–11), the Heat lost 125–95, their most lopsided loss of the year and their fourth loss in five games. In their next game against the Bulls, the Heat had a 12-point lead in the first half but ended up losing 87–86 after two failed shots by both LeBron and Wade in the last 6 seconds of the game—the Heat's 12th and 13th consecutive missed shots with a chance to tie or lead a game in the final 10 seconds of regulation or overtime. LeBron had missed four shots in the four-game losing streak. It was the Heat's fourth straight loss and the fourth time since February 24 that year that the team had lost after a double-digit lead. The Heat was 2–5 since the All-Star break, 5–13 in games decided by five or fewer points, and 14–18 against teams with winning records. Things went from bad to worse when, after the game against the Spurs, there were reports of players crying in the locker room.

Despite all the setbacks, the Heat did have many bright spots as well. On March 27, 2010, LeBron, Wade, and Bosh became the second trio in NBA history to achieve at least 30 points and 10 rebounds in the same non-overtime game. The Heat's 58-win total was the third highest in the team's history. Miami fans continued to be unimpressed, however, as the Heat ranked fifth in the NBA in overall attendance behind the Mavericks, the Cavaliers, the Trail Blazers, and the Bulls.

LeBron may not have won the league MVP that year, but he still had another amazing season with his new team and surroundings. He averaged 26.7 points, with 7 assists and 7.5 rebounds, and contributed an incredible 1.6 steals per game. He was as good as ever, and he was ready for the playoffs.

Round one came against the lowly Philadelphia 76ers. The Miami Heat was the heavy favorite—and with very good reason, easily disposing of the 76ers in five games with a 4–1 series win. LeBron was in his normal dominant playoff mode, averaging 24.2 points per game throughout the series.

Up next was an old thorn in LeBron's side: Eastern Conference champions the Boston Celtics. The series was packed with drama despite the overall dominance of the Heat, who won the series in only five games. After winning the first two at home in Miami, the Heat dropped game three in Boston before winning a dramatic overtime game four in Boston and a come-from-behind victory at home in game five to finish the series. After the series win against the Celtics, the Heat celebrated like they had won the world title, with confetti falling from the roof of the American Airlines Arena in Miami. However, the Heat still had two rounds to go if they were going to win it all.

The Eastern Conference championship series was against league MVP Derrick Rose and the top-seeded Chicago Bulls. Once again, LeBron willed the team back after a game-one loss in Chicago to win the next four games straight and a chance to take the series. During game five in Chicago, the Heat made a historic comeback after being down 77–65. With 3 minutes and 14 seconds left on the clock, the Heat went on an 18–3 run to win the game 83–80, capped by a key 4-point play from Wade and clutch shooting by LeBron.

For the first time since 2007, the Chosen One was making his way back to the NBA Finals. Serious drama was set to unfold as the Heat prepared to take on the Dallas Mavericks of the Western Conference—a rematch of the 2006 NBA Finals that the Heat had won in six games. Both teams were loaded with talent, and some believed that Dallas would give the Heat a run for its money despite Miami being heavily favored with the homecourt advantage.

The nation was locked in to this series: ABC averaged a 10.1 rating, 11.7 million households, and nearly 17.3 million viewers with the 2011 NBA Finals, according to Nielsen. In game one, Dallas's staunch defense held Miami in check, with the Heat shooting 28.6 in the first quarter. Dallas continued to play good defense and held an 8-point lead early into the third quarter until Miami finally woke up and started to make a comeback. The Heat went on a 22–10 third-quarter run and took the lead, 65–61, heading into the fourth quarter. Miami rode a 24-point performance from LeBron to win game one by a score of 92–84.

Game two turned into an instant classic as the Heat dominated for three-and-a-half quarters to hold an impressive 15-point lead with only 6 minutes to go in the game. As ABC went to a commercial break, LeBron and Wade met at half court to celebrate their for-sure victory. The Heat thought the game was over and took their foot off the gas— and that was when everything changed. Dallas began a furious rally, cutting into the lead drastically and quickly with Dirk Nowitzki leading the way. The Mavericks managed to tie the game and then take the lead as Nowitzki hit a three-point shot with 26.7 seconds left, giving Dallas a 93–90 lead. Miami was not done yet, however, as Mario Chalmers tied it up with another three-point shot at 24.5 seconds left when Jason Terry left him wide open. The veteran-loaded Dallas roster remained calm and went back to work with a play to run the clock down and shoot for the win. Jason Kidd ran the clock down then passed to Nowitzki, who made a driving layup with an injured left hand, leaving 3.6 seconds left. The Heat had no time-outs left, and Wade's potential game-winning three-pointer hit the back rim at the buzzer as he fell to the ground in an attempt to draw a foul on Nowitzki.

The immediate question was, why didn't LeBron take the final shot? But LeBron also had a poor fourth quarter performance and finished with 20 points. Wade did the majority of the scoring that game, leading the Heat with 29 points. The Mavericks' 15-point comeback was the biggest in an NBA Finals game since the 36-point comeback the Celtics had made against the Lakers in game four of the 2008 NBA Finals. The Mavericks' win broke the Heat's nine home-game winning streak in the playoffs and showed that the Heat was mortal and could collapse even after leading by 15 points late in a game.

The series shifted to Dallas for game three. Miami was still sore from the collapse in game three and came out all guns blazing to take a 7-point lead after the first quarter and a 5-point lead at the half. The Mavericks did their best to fight back from a late 14-point Miami Heat lead. With 39.6 seconds left in the fourth quarter, LeBron found Chris Bosh for a 20-foot baseline jumper. The Mavericks tried to respond as Nowitzki had a chance to force overtime, but they missed a well-defended fadeaway at the buzzer, and the Heat hung on for the win and the 2–1 series lead. LeBron scored 17 points, the least out of the Big Three with another subpar fourth quarter, and 9 assists.

Game four was the proverbial tide-hanger: LeBron pulled the ultimate disappearing act and only scored 8 points. Game four was a tight-knit affair that saw 12 lead changes and 15 ties. Early in the fourth quarter, it looked like Miami was finally going to be able to pull away from Dallas when Haslem hit a baseline jump shot to give the Heat a 74–65 lead—the largest of the game. Dallas came roaring back with the help of sharp shooter Jason Terry and actually took the lead with a little more than 5 minutes remaining in the game. As LeBron continued to go flat, the Mavericks held an 82–81 lead with 20 seconds left. Wade missed one of two free throws, which allowed Nowitzki to hit a driving layup with 14.4 seconds left to extend the lead to 3 points. After a dunk by Wade with 9 seconds left, Dallas was able to answer with two free throws by Terry to push the lead back up again to 3. The Heat still had a chance to tie the game if they could get an open look at a three-point shot. Spoelstra called a play for Wade, who fumbled the inbounds pass with 6.7 seconds left, only to make a diving save to prevent a backcourt violation. The ball landed in the hands of Mike Miller, who in desperation shot an air ball at the buzzer, preserving Dallas's 86–83 win. Once again, fans and the media were left wondered why a play for LeBron was not called in such a vital situation.

Suddenly the series was even again, and LeBron was under extreme media scrutiny because he was falling apart in the fourth quarters of games. Game five in Dallas was pivotal, as it became a best-of-three series and was the last home game in the series for Dallas. The Mavericks were red-hot from beyond the three-point line, connecting 13 times out of their 19 tries from the three-point range. Jason Terry, Jason Kidd, and "J. J." Barea combined to make 10 of those 13 three-pointers. It didn't stop Wade from doing everything he could to help Miami try to win—he ran into Brian Cardinal and had to go to the locker room with a hip injury, but he eventually returned and hit a three-pointer to cap a 9–0 run that put Miami in front, 99–95, with less than 5 minutes left in the game.

Even more drama was unfolding on the Dallas sidelines as Mavericks coach Rick Carlisle, unhappy with Terry for missing a defensive assignment and setting a poor cross-screen, pulled Terry from the game, telling him, "Refocus. I'm putting you right back in." After less than a minute, Carlisle subbed in Terry and made the crucial decision to run the offense through him for the rest of the game. This move ignited the Dallas offense while leading them on a 15–3 run in which Terry scored or assisted on 11 points. With Miami leading 100–97, Terry passed to Nowitzki, who drew a double team and then kicked it back out to Terry for a game-tying three-pointer. But the comeback wasn't over with yet: Dallas got the ball back after a stop, and Nowitzki then drove to the baseline on Bosh for a two-handed dunk with 2 minutes and 44 seconds left in the game, giving the Mavericks a 102–100 lead they would not relinquish.

On the next possession, LeBron was called for charging, giving the ball back to Dallas. Terry found Kidd wide open for another three-pointer that gave the Mavericks a 105–100 lead with 1 minute and 26 seconds remaining. The Mavericks continued to increase the lead with every possession and ended up winning the game 112–103, taking an important 3–2 lead in the series. LeBron pulled off a triple-double with 17 points, 10 assists, and 10 rebounds. It was a great triple-double, but his lack of scoring in the fourth quarter remained the major story.

As game six approached back in Miami, a panic started to take over the Heat and their fans. Who could have possibly thought the team would ever be on the verge of elimination after cruising through the majority of the season and playoffs? LeBron knew he had a lot to prove if he was going to answer his critics, and he came out gunning with his best ammo: He made his first four shots in game six to contribute to the Heat taking a 20–11 lead.

The Mavericks called a time-out and decided to rethink things; it was time for them to make needed adjustments before the game got out of reach. The Mavericks went to a zone defense that stifled Miami, with Dallas going on a 21–4 run in a span of 5 minutes and 30 seconds. Dallas made 9 of 12 shots during this stretch, with DeShawn Stevenson making two threes in a 24-second duration to give Dallas a 40–28 lead with 9 minutes and 42 seconds left in the first half. The run stunned Miami and gave Dallas the momentum on the road that they needed in a closeout game. However, LeBron and the Heat were not done fighting and went on a 14–0 run to take a 42–40 lead with 6 minutes and 25 seconds left in the half. Tempers flared as the dramatic series took a toll on the players', the fans', and the media's emotions. As the first half came to a close, Stevenson, along with Haslem and Chalmers, received technical fouls after a scuffle occurred at midcourt during a time-out. It was a wild scene and proved the stress and drama of the series was getting to everyone.

Once again, LeBron "disappeared"—he failed to score in the second half until he made a layup with 1 minute and 49 seconds remaining in the third. The Mavericks led by 9 going into the fourth quarter and increased their lead to 12 points a few minutes into the fourth. The Mavericks kept the pressure on and led by 9 with a little more than 2 minutes remaining. Time was running out on the Heat, and their fans had already left the building instead of sticking around to support the team. The Mavericks didn't allow the Heat to sneak back in the game and finished off the so-called dream team with a 105–95 series-clinching win. It was the Mavericks' first championship win in franchise history, and Dirk Nowitzki was named MVP of the series. LeBron led the Heat with 21 points, but it was far too little, far too late. The referees did everything they could to help the Heat, but it didn't matter. The officiating was so lopsided that the Heat had taken 20 more foul shots than the Mavericks. If only Miami had made their foul shots, the outcome would have been different.

Kenny Roda gave his take on why the Heat lost that series: "LeBron and the Cavs were up 2–1 the prior year and lost to Boston. The Heat were up 2–1 in that series and lost; maybe there [are] maturity issues with him that led to each letdown. Maybe they thought they had the series won and they let up both times."

Jerry Mires had a slightly different take: "The Mavericks were the better team. That was the biggest part of it. It was the Heat's first year together, and that was the same reason they started 8–7. It's not fantasy basketball, and it's not a video game where you can stack a team and just roll to victory. They were each used to being 'the guy,' so it was going to take awhile. Regular-season victories don't mean anything when you make it to the playoffs. When you get under the pressure of the Finals, you revert to your base, and those guys simply weren't together yet."

It was a shock to many fans and those in the media—few believed any team could beat the Miami Heat more than once in a series, let alone four times. It was a crushing blow for the "Big Three." Chris Bosh was so upset that he broke down crying after the game. Fans in Cleveland celebrated as if they had won a championship. It was a good-versus-evil feeling.

In a press conference after game six, LeBron didn't help his cause when he directed some harsh comments toward the Cleveland fans who had been rooting against him: "At the end of the day, all the people who want to see me fail, they gotta wake up tomorrow and have the same life they had when they woke up today. Same personal problems they had today. I am going to continue to live and do the things I want to do and be happy with that!" It was a particularly thoughtless thing to say when so many Americans were enduring rough economic times.

The only thing that could help LeBron grow up and improve his game—both on and off the court—was a visit from "The Dream."

CHAPTER EIGHT

The Champion

The Heat management spent the following off-season trying its best to recruit players to strengthen the dream team that had failed to win the 2011 NBA Championship, and they made a splash on draft night when the team traded with Chicago for Norris Cole, a point guard from Cleveland State University. Cole, a hot prospect out of Dunbar High School in Dayton, Ohio, had led his team to back-to-back state championships in his final two years.

Cole went on to a terrific four-year career at Cleveland State, where he excelled on both sides of the ball. In his senior year, Cole averaged 21.7 points, 5.8 rebounds, 5.3 assists, and 2.2 steals per game, highlighted by a 41-point, 20-rebound, 9-assist performance against Youngstown State University. He was the first person in Horizon League Men's Basketball Tournament history to be named both Player of the Year and Defensive Player of the Year. Cole was a big draft-night pickup who would supply the Heat with a solid backup point-guard option for Mario Chalmers.

Cole began the preseason strong and impressed his teammates in the annual Red and Black Intersquad Scrimmage game. He scored

21 points with 4 assists in the scrimmage and dazzled coaches with his hustle and quickness. Cole continued to turn heads throughout the preseason, with a stellar performance in which he averaged 9.5 points and 4.5 assists.

The other big off-season addition was Shane Battier. He was a 10-year veteran at the time and had once been one of the league's most explosive scorers after coming out of Duke University, where he was part of the 2001 National Championship team with Carlos Boozer. Battier was the first and only basketball player to have ever won both the Naismith Prep Player of the Year Award and the Naismith College Player of the Year (2001). After the conclusion of his college career, Battier was named to the Atlantic Coast Conference's 50th Anniversary Men's Basketball Team. Battier was also a two-time Academic All-American and was named Academic All-American of the Year in 2001. He had spent the first half of his pro career with the Memphis Grizzlies and the second half with the Houston Rockets. Battier was a viable scoring threat off the bench and brought additional veteran leadership to the Heat's team of young superstars. He was a champion at every level and a major pickup for Miami.

Opening night of the 2011–12 season for the Heat was a success with a flavor of revenge—they crushed the Dallas Mavericks in Dallas by a score of 105–94. The Heat's home opener against the Boston Celtics was a bit of a different story, though, because the men in green pushed Miami to the limit. Miami snuffed out the Celtics' comeback with their newly obtained red-hot rookie: Norris Cole helped put the Celtics away by scoring 14 points in the fourth quarter, showing his killer instinct right away, and finished with 20 points, 4 assists, 4 rebounds, and 3 steals. It was a great first night for Cole in front of the home crowd of fans. The Heat remained hot and won its first five games of the season. The team continued to look impressive and held a 15–5 record through the first 20 games.

LeBron had met with Hakeem Olajuwon in the off-season, and it was clear that the tutelage from "The Dream" was having an immediate impact on LeBron's game. He was on fire every night and clearly took over as team leader from Wade on every level, that much was clear. LeBron was dominating the league, and after 40 games, the Heat held an impressive 31–9 record. LeBron and the Heat were on a mission, and it didn't appear that anyone or any team could come close to stopping them.

Cole continued to impress; he would come off the bench with Shane Battier, Mike Miller, and others to provide the perfect spark. In the 2012 Rising Stars Challenge at the All-Star Break, Cole scored 18 points, dished out 6 assists, and swiped 4 steals in the game. He continually played his best when the spotlight was on him.

With the fast 31–9 start to the season, it looked like a sure thing that the Heat would wrap up the number-one seed quickly, but a cold streak hit instead, and the team went 15–11 in its final 26 games. That was good enough to capture the second best-record in the East, but for the second straight year, it was the Chicago Bulls earning the number-one spot.

The Miami Heat headed back to the playoffs, and once again LeBron won the MVP award—his third overall and his first as a member of the Heat. It was clear that his time with the "dream team" had helped, as LeBron was now beyond a shadow of a doubt the best player on the planet. He had worked hard to earn the honor and had chosen to ignore the critics around him.

The 2012 NBA Playoffs were the second time the Miami Heat's Big Three were brought under the spotlight. Fans and the nation wondered if LeBron could finally get over the hump and begin producing the championships he promised at the pep rally the year before. The Heat would have one less thing to worry about right away, because the best player on the number one–seeded Chicago Bulls went down with a season-ending injury on the very first day of the playoffs: Derrick Rose was left in a blowout game far too long against the Philadelphia 76ers and tore his ACL. It was a fatal blow for the 50-game-winning Bulls that caused them to eventually lose the first-round series against the lowly 76ers, who had won only 35 games.

At first it seemed that Rose's injury would give the Heat an open door to the NBA Finals—the team crushed the New York Knicks in five games in the opening round and got off to a 1–0 series lead against their round-two opponents, the Indiana Pacers. The game-one win didn't come without sacrifice, however; Chris Bosh hurt his back and would be unable to return for the rest of the series. The Pacers won game two 78–75 as the Heat coughed up a late lead, and without Bosh, Miami seemed to be losing momentum. Game three was the worst in playoff history for Wade: He scored only 5 points on 2 of 13 shooting, and the Heat found themselves in a 2–1 hole after a 94–75 blowout loss.

With the media suddenly counting out the Heat and discussing the potential of Miami having to blow up the Big Three, the team responded with a great game four to draw even in the series. Wade bounced back and scored 30 points in the 101–93 win. However, it was LeBron capturing the headlines with a marvelous effort, scoring 40 points, pulling down 18 rebounds, and dishing out 9 assists. The Pacers blew their chance to put the Heat away and never recovered. The Heat won the next two games easily and knocked the Indiana Pacers out of the series—an event that would soon become a familiar trend in the two team's budding rivalry.

It was high drama as the Heat's familiar rivals, the Boston Celtics, came to town looking for revenge after getting taken out by Miami in the previous season. Game one was the typical Miami Heat blowout, with the Celtics attempting a comeback at one point, but the Heat just had too much fire power. LeBron was his usual stellar self, scoring 32 points with 13 rebounds.

Game two provided thrills and serious drama throughout the entire game. Boston started off hot and jumped out to a 15-point lead. The Heat came roaring back in the second quarter and cut the lead down to 7 points at the half. The Heat then went on a run that saw them take a 6-point lead heading into the final frame. With the team down 3 and only 34 seconds left in the game, it was Allen who hit a clutch three-pointer to tie the game at 99. LeBron had two chances to win the game for Miami in regulation but couldn't convert, and the gamed headed into overtime. Rajon Rondo played the game of his life that night, scoring 44 points with 10 assists, but it wasn't enough for the Celtics, as the Heat won 115–111. Boston complained of poor officiating as the Heat shot 18 more free throws, the Celtics committed 33 fouls to the Heat's 18, and when the game was tied in overtime, Rondo was hit in the head by Wade with no foul called, leading to a fast-break dunk for Haslem.

The series took on a feel of desperation for the Celtics as they headed back home for game three. LeBron wanted to put Boston away before they could scratch their way back into the series. He came out blazing, scoring 16 points and making 7 of his first 9 shots. The Celtics answered LeBron's efforts with their own round of fire and outscored the Heat 55–35 in the second and third quarters and held an 85–63 lead heading into the fourth. Despite a late rally by the Heat, the Celtics managed to hold on and win 101–91. LeBron continued his playoff dominance with a 34-point and 8-rebound effort in the loss. A great game for LeBron resulting in a loss for his team because of poor support was not an uncommon theme in his career.

Game four was another overtime thriller, the second in the series in just its first four games. The Celtics led at one point by as many as 18 points, but the Heat, led by LeBron, came storming back and forced the extra frame, with LeBron hitting a three-pointer with 36 seconds left in regulation. It was clear that he was moving past any previous postseason demons during this run. The Heat had a big chance in over-time when the Celtics' best player, Paul Pierce, fouled out with more than 4 minutes left in overtime. But LeBron also fouled out with 1 minute and 51 seconds left, and it became anyone's game. With the Celtics clinging to a 2-point lead in the final seconds, Erik Spoelstra drew up a play that ended in Wade taking a desperation three-pointer that ultimately missed and tied the series. LeBron took serious crit-icism for fouling out in overtime with still so much time left in the game, even though he led the Heat in scoring with 29 points.

The series was quickly turning into a classic, and game five wouldn't disappoint. The series returned to Miami with two games apiece. The Heat would once again have the services of the return-ing Chris Bosh; it was a big boost for the team, because LeBron had been doing the bulk of the work. It didn't matter, though—the Celtics remained hot and took game five on the visiting court by a score of 93–91. The key moment in this game had the Celtics leading by 1 point with less than a minute to go and Pierce knocking down a crucial three-pointer that gave the Celtics the lead for good. Coach Spoelstra took heavy criticism from the media and fans for letting Bosh play just 14 minutes total despite being productive with 9 rebounds and 7 points in that short stretch. It didn't help the coach's demeanor as he walked off the court to an obnoxious fan yelling at him, "Good game, game effort!" Despite the loss, LeBron had yet another great game with 30 points and 13 rebounds.

With the Heat's backs once again against the wall heading into the hostile TD Garden in Boston, LeBron had finally had enough and decided to win the NBA Championship by himself that season, dom-inating from start to finish in game six and scoring 45 points—30 of which were scored in the first half alone—with 15 rebounds. He never looked to pass the ball, but he simply drove it to the lane every time he touched it—an unstoppable force against Boston. LeBron had arrived:

The three-time MVP award winner had finally put a team on his back, cleared everyone else out of the way, and carried the game himself! It was a blowout 98–79 win that sent the series back to Miami for a deciding game seven.

Ken Carman later gave his take on why LeBron took over that game the way he did:

He showed that he was a different player at that point. He lived up to the expectations of being a champion; he showed what you have to be and do to win. Everybody has a learning curve, that's why we call people prodigies who don't have one. It is very rare that a person can pick something up the first time they do it and become the absolute best at it the first time they do it. You see it in music, writing, and maybe a couple of other things, and that it why it is so rare. He is a basketball prodigy in many ways. In sports there are winners and losers. In music we can be subjective as with writing and television and all these other things, but in sports there are winners and losers. There are guys in front of you that you have to beat and take it from them, and that is part of the growth process involved with it. Every single player is going to have that challenge at some point. That is what makes athletes such as Tom Brady such an incredible story because he is the best-of-the-best out of nowhere and that is the difference between sports and everything else. You just have to hit that extra gear when you have the talent, and that is what [LeBron] did in that game. I have always said guys like Peyton Manning play in the ultimate team spirit but have also been a victim of their own talent. Those around [Manning] tend to rest on their own laurels because he is so good. I think LeBron James in the NBA runs into the same thing: Those around him will rest on their laurels because he is so good. The players around him will wait for him to bail them out and we saw that constantly in Cleveland. He wasn't ready yet and didn't have that extra gear to go further, but now he does, and he proved it in that series against Boston with the Heat. Once he realized that, that is when he became a game-changer and a serious edge. It is a dangerous game, however, because eventually it will fail if you keep relying on the same thing or person. He had players around him getting old and hurt, so how much confidence was really there? If you are continuously focusing on one guy to bail you out, eventually because of time he is going to let you down at least once. LeBron didn't let anyone down in Miami, but you have to do what you can to preserve his talent and help him out! Someday, and people don't want to realize this, but someday that LeBron may be a ghost LeBron because of this constant need from him. People will figure him out over time because time will eventually catch you, so you have to make the most of the time you have now like he is doing and did that night. When you have LeBron, you need to make the most out of it: He is a once-in-a-generation superstar. He is the best player on the face of the earth. Time and time again, players of his caliber are victims of their own success because people take them for granted.

Kenny Roda also recalled the incredible effort from LeBron that evening:

It was the best performance of his career and reminded me of his dominant game in the Palace back in the 2007 Eastern Conference Finals against the Detroit Pistons in game five of a tied-up-at-two series. He scored 45 points and 30 of those were in the first half. This game extended the Heat's season and extended the run of the Big Three.

The Celtics kept game seven close all night and did everything they could to try and steal one more win from the Heat. The Celtics held an 11-point lead halfway through the second quarter despite

Garnett being on the bench with 3 fouls, and they took a 7-point lead into the locker room at halftime. It was the closest the Celtics would get to the NBA Finals, as LeBron and the Miami Heat turned things back around in their favor during the second half. The Heat came all the way back from behind and tied the game heading into the fourth. Boston continued to battle, but the fourth quarter belonged to LeBron, and the Heat pulled away with the 101–88 win to head to the 2012 NBA Finals.

LeBron had always had issues with the Celtics in the past, and now he had beaten them for the second straight season. Unlike the year before, however, this season was all business, and the Heat managed to keep their eye on the prize. They were still shell-shocked from blowing the 2–1 series lead the year before, and they were determined not to let it happen again.

In contrast to the previous year, the Heat would now be the slight underdog because they had to start the series on the road against Western Conference Champions the Oklahoma City Thunder. The Thunder had its own group of superstars and was considered a serious threat to take down LeBron and crew.

Oklahoma City was led by one of the best players in the game, Kevin Durant. The 6-foot-9-inch-tall, 240-pound small forward was one of the quickest and sharpest players in the game. He could score at will and put the Thunder back in any game despite any deficit they might be facing.

Durant grew up around the game and was a superstar at a young age, having played Amateur Athletic Union basketball while growing up in the Maryland area. The competition was stiff in the AAU, but he was teammates with future NBA players Michael Beasley and Ty Lawson, and together the three of them grew into great talents through AAU ball. The young Durant also showed maturity and compassion beyond his years when, during this time, he began wearing 35 as his jersey number in honor of his AAU coach Charles Craig, who was murdered at the age of 35.

Durant was highly touted coming out of high school. He attended National Christian Academy for his first two years, then transferred to the famous Oak Hill Academy, which has produced numerous NBA superstars, most famously Carmelo Anthony. Durant transferred again for his senior year, this time to Montrose Christian School. It was a year of growth, both figuratively and literally, for Durant, who had grown 5 inches before the start of his senior season and began the year at a height of 6 feet 9 inches. And aside from his height, his overall athletic ability was unusual for a senior in high school.

Durant's senior year was a giant success. He was named the *Washington Post* All-Met Basketball Player of the Year. He continued to show he could play with the best and beat the best when he was named MVP of the 2006 McDonald's All-American Game. He was one of the top five high school prospects in 2006. He had the talent to leap straight to the NBA, but the new rules no longer allowed that so he had to go to college for at least one dominant year. Before the start of his senior season, Durant committed to the University of Texas. The Longhorns were happy about the new NBA rule and were ecstatic to have him in uniform.

Durant didn't mess around, making the most out of his one season at Texas. During his time as a Longhorn, he averaged 25.8 points, 11.1 rebounds, and 1.3 assists per game. He helped lead the team to a great season, and they finished the year with a 25–10 record overall and a 12–4 record in conference. Thanks to his performance, the Longhorns were named the fourth seed in the NCAA Tournament. Durant led them past New Mexico State in the first round before they got knocked out in the second round by the University of Southern California. Durant had won numerous awards that season, the most prestigious being the Naismith College Player of the Year—he was the first-ever freshman to win the award. So memorable and remarkable was his one year at Texas that a few short years later, the university retired his jersey.

At the time of the 2007 NBA draft, the Seattle SuperSonics were in a state of transition as they were about to play their final season in Seattle before moving to Oklahoma City. Durant was taken second by the SuperSonics (the only player picked in front of him was eventual draft bust Greg Oden). The Seattle fans would not get to see Durant for very long, but what they did see was well worth it. It wasn't very long until Durant was the leading scorer and making buzzer-beater shots to win games in a thrilling fashion. His first pro success came less than a month into the season, when he hit a last-second winning shot against the Atlanta Hawks. So impressive was his rookie season that, despite the SuperSonics lackluster season, Durant was still able to achieve Rookie of the Year honors. He joined LeBron James and Carmelo Anthony as the only teenagers in the history of the NBA to average more than 20 points a game. His final stat line for the season was 20.3 points per game with 4.4 rebounds and 2.4 assists—solid numbers for the popular rookie.

Following Durant's debut season, the Sonics relocated from Seattle to Oklahoma City, becoming the Thunder and playing in front of packed houses with ravenous fans just happy to have a basketball team at the pro level to watch. The first year in Oklahoma City saw the Thunder draft Russell Westbrook, a high-scoring point guard out of UCLA. P. J. Carlesimo was the head coach for the Thunder's first 13 games that season, but after a 1–12 start he was fired and replaced by Scott Brooks. Brooks didn't fare much better—the team went 22–47 the rest of the season under his direction. However, fans could tell that the team had a good, young nucleus starting to build. One major highlight was at the All-Star Weekend during the rookies-versus-sophomores game, in which Durant set a record with

46 points. By the end of the year, he had raised his scoring average by 5 points from the previous season to 25.3 points per game, and he was considered a strong candidate for the NBA Most Improved Player Award, eventually finishing third in the voting.

Durant's partner in crime for most breakaway dunks was rookie sensation Russell Westbrook. The young point guard averaged 15.3 points, 5.3 assists, 4.9 rebounds, and 1.3 steals that season. He finished fourth in the 2008–09 NBA Rookie of the Year voting behind eventual Rookie of the Year Derrick Rose. Westbrook was a West Coast kid who grew up on the basketball court instead of the beach; he spent his time idolizing the likes of Magic Johnson. Westbrook's game was like Johnson's in that he could shoot and pass with ease. Unlike Durant, Westbrook was not highly touted in high school—he didn't start on his school's varsity team at Leuzinger High School until his junior year, and he didn't receive his first college recruiting letter until the summer before his senior year. Like Durant, Westbrook showed his ability to take charge in his senior year when he led his team to a 25–4 overall record and to a California Interscholastic Federation Southern Section Division I-AA quarterfinal playoff appearance. Despite not getting recruited heavily, Westbrook still had solid numbers, averaging 25.1 points, 8.7 rebounds, 3.1 steals, and 2.3 assists. He collected 14 double-doubles, scored 30 or more points on eight occasions, and registered a career-best 51 points. Shockingly, he received few scholarships, but after Jordan Farmar left UCLA for the pros, head coach Ben Howland decided to bring Westbrook into the fold.

Westbrook's days at UCLA were good, and he was able to improve each season. His freshman year, he learned behind starting guard Darren Collison and received most of his time as a defensive specialist. The following season, Westbrook would earn his big chance as Collison went down to injury. He made the most of that chance by averaging 12.7 points, 3.9 rebounds, 4.7 assists, and 1.6 steals. At the end of the year, Westbrook was named All-Pacific-10 Third Team and won the Pacific-10 Defensive Player of the Year award. Westbrook only played college ball for two years, but UCLA advanced to the Final Four during both of Westbrook's seasons with the team. In 2007, UCLA lost 76–66 to eventual national champions the University of Florida, and in 2008, they lost 78–63 to the University of Memphis. Westbrook declared for the draft shortly thereafter.

The Thunder stepped it up in the 2009–10 season as Westbrook became a full-time starter and went on to average 16.1 points, 8 assists, and 4.9 rebounds per game that season. The Scott Brooks–led Thunder showed amazing improvement, increasing their victory total by winning 27 more games than the year before. They eventually lost to the Los Angeles Lakers in the first round, but battling the Lakers close caught the rest of the league's attention—many in the media were starting to mention the Thunder as a future title contender.

The 2010–11 year was a breakout one for the Oklahoma City Thunder. They won a franchise best (at the time) 55 games, which was good enough to capture the team the Northwest Division title. Durant and Westbrook really started to jell and become one of the top duos in the NBA. Durant, fresh off of signing a five-year contract extension for $86 million, averaged 27.7 points a game. It was the second consecutive year that Durant was able to take home the scoring title for the season. In the playoffs, Oklahoma City defeated the Denver Nuggets and the Memphis Grizzlies en route to a Conference Finals match-up versus the Dallas Mavericks. The Thunder was getting closer by the season.

When the strike of 2011 rolled around, it bit no two teams worse than the Heat and the Thunder, because teams were so loaded with potential and felt they had unfinished business from the year before. Durant was on a mission from day one of the strike-shortened season, including a 51-point performance against the Denver Nuggets early in the season. At the 2012 All-Star Game, Durant scored 36 points and was awarded his first All-Star Game MVP Award. His magical season only continued, as he averaged 28 points per game that helped him achieve his third straight scoring title.

The Thunder's 47 wins were good enough for the second-best record in the Western Conference. However, Oklahoma City had their hands full in the playoffs that season because they had to get through Dallas, the defending NBA Champions in the opening round. Durant once again showed he had ice in his veins when he hit the game-winning shot with only 1.5 seconds remaining during opening night of the playoffs against the defending NBA Champions. The Thunder won another nail-biter in game two by a score of 102–99 to take a commanding lead on the road to Dallas. Durant and Westbrook continued to show their dominance and emergence in the league as they blew out the Mavericks in game three at 95–79. Their last true test was in game four when the Thunder trailed by 13 points heading into the final quarter. Durant and Westbrook once again stepped up and led the charge for a 35–16 run, eventually winning the game 103–97 and knocking out the Dallas Mavericks.

The Los Angeles Lakers promised to be a tougher test in the second round for the young Thunder team. It was a showdown between the best players in the Western Conference: Kobe Bryant against the team on the rise. The combination of Durant and Westbrook was too much for the Lakers to handle—each game was dominated by the dynamic duo. The Lakers managed to scratch out a victory in game three, but other than that, the series belonged to the Thunder. In each game, the leading scorers, rebounders, and assists were Durant and Westbrook.

Many thought that the young group would finally be stopped by the veteran-laden San Antonio Spurs in the 2012 Western Conference

Finals. Kevin Durant had other ideas, though, putting on a scoring display in all six games. The Spurs jumped out to a 2–0 lead in the series before the Thunder kicked things into high gear. The Thunder used the red-hot Durant, with point totals of 27, 31, 22, 36, 27, and 34, to come back and defeat the Spurs 4–2 in the series, setting up the dream match between Durant and LeBron. Years earlier, the NBA offices had prayed for a LeBron-versus-Kobe Finals but were disappointed when the Orlando Magic stunned the Cleveland Cavaliers. The NBA got their wish this time, however, as their new top two names were set to go head-to-head in the NBA Finals. LeBron was fresh off of winning the MVP award for the third time in four years, and Durant was the fastest rising star in all of sports, along with being a multiple-time scoring champion. The NBA Finals were sure to have fireworks once again!

NBA Western Conference champions the Oklahoma City Thunder were led by youthful coach Scott Brooks. He had been around the game the majority of his life and was the right man to lead the Thunder into this crucial series. Brooks played prep basketball at East Union High School in Manteca, California, in 1983. After graduating from high school, he enrolled at Texas Christian University but played just one season there before transferring to San Joaquin Delta College in Stockton, California. When he was unable to earn a spot on the basketball team there, the determined Brooks once again moved schools, this time landing at the University of California, Irvine. It was a smart choice: In his senior season, he averaged 23.8 points and made 43.2 percent of his three-point attempts. Brooks will be forever remembered for the opening game at the Bren Events Center, where he christened the team's new home arena with an epic performance, scoring 43 points as UCI defeated Utah State 118–96 on January 8, 1997.

Despite not being drafted by any NBA teams out of college, Brooks had a passion for the game and decided to play for the Albany

Patroons of the Continental Basketball Association. He quickly proved NBA scouts wrong for not picking him: He was named to the CBA's All-Rookie Team in 1988 and was a member of Albany's CBA Championship team that same season. Shortly after that, he realized his dream of playing in the NBA and went on to play for the Philadelphia 76ers, the Minnesota Timberwolves, the Houston Rockets, the Dallas Mavericks, the New York Knicks, and the Cleveland Cavaliers; he also became a member of Houston's 1994 NBA Championship team. When the Los Angeles Clippers released Brooks in October 1999 during the 1999–2000 preseason, his NBA career as a player ended, but he was not done with the game. Brooks joined the Los Angeles Stars of the American Basketball Association in 2000–01, serving as both a player and an assistant coach.

Brooks brought his coaching skills to the NBA when, after serving as an assistant coach with the Sacramento Kings and Denver Nuggets, he was named an assistant to head coach Carlesimo with the Seattle SuperSonics before the 2007–08 season and followed the team to Oklahoma City to become the Thunder following that season. When Carlesimo was fired on November 22, 2008, Brooks was named interim coach for the rest of the season. On April 22, 2009, Oklahoma City decided to hire him full-time.

It didn't take Brooks long to reward the Thunder's faith in him. He was named the 2009–2010 NBA Coach of the Year after leading the Thunder to a 50-win season and the eighth seed in the Western Conference for the playoffs, a 26-win increase over the previous season. Brooks was the perfect man to lead the high-energy, fast-paced Thunder in their collision course against the Miami Heat.

Game one of the 2012 NBA Finals, on June 12, 2012, took place in front of a packed house of screaming fans in Oklahoma City. It was unheard of for a franchise so young in its history to reach the championship. LeBron was still hated by many fans and the media for his handling of the Cleveland departure, and because of this, Oklahoma City became the sentimental favorite to win. The only two cities rooting for the Heat were Miami and Seattle.

The Miami Heat were out to prove their prior year's loss to the Dallas Mavericks was a fluke, and that their "Big Three" were indeed capable of multiple championships. The Heat came out firing on all cylinders, hitting 5 three-pointers in the first quarter as LeBron led the charge. Miami held a 13-point lead in the second quarter, and the Thunder were on the verge of getting blown out. However, the Thunder managed to fight back and keep the game close; Miami led just 54–47 at the end of the first half. The tide changed in the second half with strong plays from Durant and Westbrook as the Thunder took the lead to close out the third quarter, 74–73. Kevin Durant was on his way to a 36-point game while his teammate Westbrook finished with 27 points. LeBron, who had a stellar first three quarters and finished the game with 30 total points, once again had a tragic fourth quarter and failed to score in the final until only 4 minutes remained in the contest. Wade helped out with 8 assists, but it wasn't enough, and the Heat lost their fourth straight NBA Finals game, 105–94. The Heat needed to regroup, and quickly.

In the postgame press conference LeBron seemed calm, as if he knew it was just a matter of time before the Heat figured things out and turned it around. Heading into game two, Miami knew it would be a tall task to overcome the Thunder, as the young team still hadn't lost a playoff game at home. For the second straight game, the Heat jumped out to a big lead: They led by 12 at the end of the first quarter and maintained that advantage heading into the locker room at halftime. Despite a 32-point performance from Durant, the combination of LeBron and Bosh proved to be too much for the Thunder to handle. LeBron scored 32 points, while Bosh ripped down 15 boards. The Thunder made it close and Durant had a chance to tie it in the closing seconds, but they failed—the Heat hung on to win 100–96, tying the series at one game apiece headed back to Miami.

As the series continued into game three, the Heat knew they could take a serious advantage with the win and put themselves in a prime position going forward if they could avoid the letdown after the big win. The first half was hotly contested and tightly played, but Miami held a razor-thin 1-point lead heading into halftime. The Thunder came out of the locker room scoring on every position and quickly built a 10-point lead on the Heat. To their credit, the Heat could have folded again, but LeBron started to carry his teammates on his shoulders and brought them right back into the game; they scored the last 7 points in the third quarter to regain the lead at 69–67.

The Heat fell behind by a point midway through the fourth before LeBron once again brought the Heat back and led them on an 8–0 run to give Miami an 84–77 lead with 3 minutes and 47 seconds left in the game. Then the Thunder mustered a quick 6-point run and brought the game to within 1 point at 84–83 with only 1 minute and 30 seconds remaining. It was at this point that the Heat played the amazing defense they had been playing all season to shut down the Thunder for the rest of the game, meanwhile converting 5 straight foul shots to win game three 91–85 and take a 2–1 lead in the series. LeBron was amazing again, scoring 29 points while capturing 14 rebounds.

It was at this point the year before that LeBron started to crumble, as the Heat held a 2–1 lead and began to let it slip away. Two years earlier, with the Cavaliers against Boston, LeBron saw it happen there as well. It was pivotal to the Heat that they come out strong and avoid another game-four meltdown. The Heat knew that if they could just win game four, they would be in the driver's seat to close out the series.

The Thunder had other plans, though. They started the game like a desperate team in need of a win; they knew a loss would be backbreaking at this point. The Thunder raced out to a 33–19 lead after the first quarter, but as usual, LeBron led the Miami Heat right back into the game and cut the lead to 49–46 headed into the half. LeBron and the Heat were not to be denied!

The Miami Heat and the Oklahoma Thunder stood toe-to-toe in the third quarter and exchanged haymakers like two heavyweight prizefighters. The Miami Heat was able to secure a small 4-point lead heading into the final frame. The main problem for the Thunder was that one of its best players, James Harden, was having the worst series of his life. Harden played miserably and looked lost out there most of the time—like a kid who was scared to get caught with his hand in the cookie jar—and became a turnover machine every time he touched the ball. Despite a huge effort by Durant and Westbrook, who scored 28 points and 43 points, respectively, the Thunder couldn't get past Harden's horrendous play that night.

The Miami Heat capitalized on the garbage plays by Harden and had several players help LeBron to put the game away. Chalmers scored 25 points and made two key plays to seal Miami's win. To go along with the great play by Chalmers, LeBron was able to score 26 points, pass for 12 assists, and rebound 9 missed shots. He was the team leader in each category and just one win short of an NBA title as the Heat put the Thunder away 104–94. LeBron had the go-ahead three-pointer that put the Heat on top for good, but he had to miss the last 2 minutes of the game due to leg cramps. It didn't cost him or his team that night, but soon enough the cramps would return to cost "King James" his throne.

On June 21, 2012, LeBron finally began to put away the distraction of the flack for his decision to leave Cleveland and move past the demons that had been haunting him. The Miami Heat won the NBA Championship with another amazing effort by the Chosen One. LeBron put the Heat on his back and brought home the gold once and for all by dominating in game five and scoring 26 points, dishing out 13 assists, and pulling down 11 rebounds. It was an impressive triple-double that helped the Heat become the champions of the NBA world. Opposing coach Brooks never found a way to stop LeBron or inspire Harden to stop turning the ball over and help out Durant and Westbrook.

The clincher was a blowout, with Miami leading by as much as 27 at one point. Coming off the bench to light it up from the three-point range was Mike Miller, who cashed in on 7 of 8 attempts from beyond the arc. (Miller had entered the game only because Dwayne Wade encountered foul trouble in the first half.) The team tied an NBA Finals record for the most three-pointers in a game with 14 total. LeBron was named the NBA Finals MVP after averaging 28.6 points, 10.2 rebounds, and 7.4 assists in the finals. No one complained, because finally the Chosen One had reached his destiny. People could call LeBron a quitter for his performance in game five against Boston years before in Cleveland, or call him the various other mean-spirited names he earned after he left Cleveland, but none of that mattered now because the only name that meant something to LeBron was "Champion."

CHAPTER NINE

The Spurs

It had finally happened for LeBron James. After a brilliant nine-year career, three MVP awards, and countless accolades, he had reached the pinnacle of sports when he became NBA world champion. A huge weight was lifted off his shoulders, and he could spend the first part of the summer celebrating before leaving to play in the 2012 Summer Olympics with Team USA. That experience was also golden—as in the gold medal to which he led the team.

As LeBron basked in another glorious achievement, Miami began to build the defense for their crown. The Heat started their off-season by signing veteran three-point shooting specialist Ray Allen, who had been playing on the same Boston Celtics team that Miami had bounced from the playoffs the two prior years. Allen was a standout at the University of Connecticut from 1993 to 1996, where he earned All-American status and was named USA Basketball's Male Athlete of the Year in 1995. In 1995–96, Allen was a First Team All-American and won the Big East Player of the Year award. When his college career ended, Ray Allen was third all-time in scoring with 1,922 points, and he had set a single-season school record by connecting on

115 three-pointers from 1995 to 1996. His college career was so impressive that in 2001 he was named honorary captain of the 25-member UConn All-Century Basketball Team. On February 5, 2007, his name and number were honored at Connecticut's Harry A. Gampel Pavilion during the "Huskies of Honor" ceremony at halftime during the men's basketball game against the Syracuse Orange. Allen became so popular so quickly with his amazing shooting ability that he was even cast in a lead role in the Spike Lee film *He Got Game.*

Allen was drafted fifth in the 1996 NBA draft by the Minnesota Timberwolves, but he was quickly traded to the Milwaukee Bucks for the rights to fourth pick Stephon Marbury. He excelled in his rookie season as a member of the NBA's All-Rookie Second Team in 1996. It was an impressive honor for Allen because the draft class was loaded with such stars as Allen Iverson, Marcus Camby, Stephon Marbury, Antoine Walker, Kobe Bryant, Peja Stojaković, Steve Nash, Jermaine O'Neal, and Žydrūnas Ilgauskas. Some believe that Allen is part of the most talented draft class in the history of the NBA—with the sole exception of LeBron's draft class in 2003—that reshaped an entire league. His career in Milwaukee went from 1996 to 2003 and went well. The highlight of his time in Milwaukee was his amazing 2001 season when he won the three-point shootout during All-Star Weekend and was selected to the All-NBA Third Team. Alongside Sam Cassell and Glenn Robinson, Allen led the Bucks to the Eastern Conference Finals where they lost in seven games to the Allen Iverson–led Philadelphia 76ers. It was a thrilling series that saw the Bucks almost pull off the upset.

In a shocking trade midway through the 2002–03 season, Allen was dealt to the Sonics, along with Ronald Murray, former UConn teammate Kevin Ollie, and a conditional first-round draft pick in exchange for Gary Payton and Desmond Mason. The swap for Gary Payton was seen as an even exchange of two of the best guards in the entire league. Allen had a slow start with the SuperSonics because his first full season with them was hampered by injuries, but he bounced back the next season in 2004–05; he was named to the All-NBA Second Team and, alongside teammate Rashard Lewis, led the Sonics to the Conference Semifinals in 2005. Allen was recruited heavily by LeBron and the Cleveland Cavaliers following the 2005 season, but he spurned Danny Ferry and the Cavaliers and signed a five-year, $80 million contract extension. Allen proved worthy of the money in the 2006–07 regular season, averaging a career-high 26.4 points per game while adding 4.5 rebounds and 4.1 assists per game. His career with the Sonics was filled with highlights, and on March 12, 2006, Allen became the 97th player in NBA history to score 15,000 points. On April 19, 2006, Allen broke Dennis Scott's 10-year NBA record for three-point field goals made in a season in a game against the Denver Nuggets.

Heading into the 2007–08 season, the Boston Celtics were in the process of creating their Big Three, and Ray Allen was on the top of their list to bring in to play with Paul Pierce. On June 28, 2007, the Sonics traded Allen and Glen Davis, the 35th overall pick in the 2007 NBA draft, to the Celtics in exchange for Delonte West, Wally Szczerbiak, and the fifth overall pick, Jeff Green. The building continued as the Celtics acquired Minnesota Timberwolves' forward Kevin Garnett to play alongside Allen and Pierce. The Boston Celtics finished 66–16 and were the number-one seed in the 2008 NBA Playoffs. On June 17, 2008, in the series-ending game six of the NBA Finals, Allen tied an NBA Finals record with 7 three-pointers in the Celtics' 131–92 victory over the Los Angeles Lakers. Allen was now an NBA Champion for the first time and continued to play the following seasons until he became an unrestricted free agent following the 2012 regular season when the Heat pounced. It came with serious bitterness from Boston fans when Allen abandoned his teammates Garnett and Pierce to leave for the enemy.

To accompany gaining Allen, the Miami Heat also signed veteran sharp shooter Rashard Lewis. A phenom out of high school who, despite being recruited by Florida State, Kansas, and Houston, bypassed college and opted instead to go pro, Lewis was selected by the Seattle SuperSonics with the third pick in the second round of the 1998 NBA draft. In 2001, Lewis was also selected to play for the USA in the Goodwill Games, in which USA won the gold medal.

Lewis left Seattle after nine solid seasons and joined the Orlando Magic, having agreed to a six-year sign-and-trade deal worth $118 million. Lewis broke out in the 2009 season as the team's second-leading scorer, earning an appearance in the 2009 NBA All-Star Game. LeBron was all too familiar with what Lewis was capable of as, in the 2009 NBA Playoffs, Lewis hit a game-winning shot in the first game of the Eastern Conference Finals against the Cleveland Cavaliers. After a short stint in both Washington and New Orleans, Lewis was a free agent again, and the Heat brought him in to complete the roster. Lewis signed a two-year, $2.8 million deal and was also reunited with his former Seattle teammate Ray Allen. The Heat just kept getting bigger and better by the day, as if the reigning MVP and best basketball player on the planet needed the extra help, but Coach Spoelstra was happy to have it. Lewis's season would be unimpressive, however, as he played in just 55 games, starting 9 and averaging 5.2 points per game; however, Spoelstra would state many times that Lewis's defense off the bench often provided the lock-down coverage the Heat needed late in games.

The Miami Heat were loaded and ready to make a defense of their title. No one was picking against them to come out of the East as champions once again. As it often is with champions, the whole league was looking to take down the Heat, and the media was hungry for a storyline about how it could be possible for a team to do so. No such further proof was needed when, after just two games, some in the media were already questioning the Heat's dominance as they lost their second game of the season to the New York Knicks at Madison Square Garden. The Knicks crushed the Heat 104–84 as Carmelo Anthony went off for 30 points. Little-known Steve Novak came off the bench for the Knicks and scored 17 points as he nailed 5 three-pointers. In fact, as a team, the Knicks sunk a ridiculous 19 three-pointers by night's end. It started up talk immediately about the Heat's lack of defense when it came to defending the three-point shot.

The Heat responded to their critics as they rolled off four straight wins, three of them coming at home and one on the road in Atlanta. After a win at Houston was sandwiched between two losses, the Heat once again got hot and won six straight games, including one over LeBron's former team. The Heat stayed hot and, after crushing the Oklahoma City Thunder on Christmas day, they held an impressive 19–6 record.

Each night that the Heat played, the opposing teams would bring their best to try and bring Miami down. Everyone guns for the champions, and throughout the course of the year, injuries can pile up as each team plays them physical, which makes what happened next so impressive.

Starting Sunday, February 3, 2013, with a 100–85 win at Toronto, the Heat began an amazing 27-game winning streak that had everyone believing the Heat could possibly take down the NBA record set by the Los Angeles Lakers in 1971–72 when they won 33 straight games. The Heat came within six wins of pulling off the amazing record that stood for more than 40 years. Only one team during this epic streak was able to take the Heat into extra frames: the Sacramento Kings, who forced double overtime before losing. The streak ended on Wednesday, March 27, 2013, against the Chicago Bulls in Chicago at 101–97.

Before the season was over, the Heat lost only one more time, again to the New York Knicks, and won their last 11 of 12 games,

38 out of 40, to finish the season with the Eastern Conference's best record at 66–16. The second place team in their division, the Atlanta Hawks, won only 22 fewer games. The Heat was the clear-cut favorite to win the NBA Championship once again. LeBron had another incredible season, averaging 26.8 points a game with 8 rebounds a night and 7.3 assists. On top of those incredible numbers year-in and year-out, he continued to play great defense and averaged 1.7 steals per game. LeBron was the total package and the best player in the league on both sides of the ball, all signs posted to victory in the upcoming playoffs .

The Heat would need LeBron to continue his dominance as they were not sure what kind of effort they would get from Wade, who only played in 69 games that season and saw his point-per-game average drop to 21.9. Bosh also had slightly declining numbers with 16 points a game and just 6 rebounds. For LeBron to be out rebounding Bosh spoke volumes about both of their efforts.

The addition of Allen to the team paid off big as he played in 79 games and averaged 10.9 points a game. He provided a solid bench boost as he played 25 minutes a night, averaging 1.9 three-pointers a night. Cole also continued to be a solid backup option at point guard as he played a serviceable role off the bench and chipped in with 2 assists a game.

As the playoffs began, all eyes were on LeBron to see if he could carry the Heat once more to another World Championship. Their round-one series was against the lowly Milwaukee Bucks, who barely had enough talent to cover the Miami Heat's backups. To the surprise of no one, the Heat walked right through the Bucks in a dominating four-game sweep. Game one was 110–87 with LeBron scoring 27 points, pulling down 10 rebounds, and handing out 8 assists in only 34 minutes of playing time. Game two was a little closer as the Heat won 98–86. LeBron scored only 19 points but still dished out 6 assists while rebounding 8 missed shots. It was Wade stepping it up in game two with 21 points to lead the Heat. Game three was another blowout as the Heat crushed the Bucks 104–91. It was another stellar effort from LeBron, who played just 32 minutes but racked up 22 points, 5 rebounds, and 6 assists, and Allen came off the bench to crush his former team by scoring 23 points and drilling 5 three-pointers in only 30 minutes—catching fire at just the right time. LeBron took it upon himself to close things out in game four with a 30-point, 8-rebound, 3-steal, and 7-assist performance. Wade didn't even need to play—Coach Spoelstra chose to rest the aging star with his troublesome knees. The Heat beat the Bucks 88–77 and headed off to a second-round showdown with their old nemesis, the Chicago Bulls. This was the seventh playoff meeting for these two teams, with Chicago having won four of the six previous series.

The best player on the Chicago Bulls was Derrick Rose, the 2011 league MVP. The problem was that he hadn't played a single minute since game one of the 2012 playoffs, when he tore his ACL. All season long, the talk had been about his possible comeback in time for the playoffs. However, when the playoffs finally arrived, he still couldn't play, even though the doctors were giving him full medical clearance to do so. The Chicago fans were not happy with their superstar, whom they badly needed heading into this crucial series against the league's best team. The entire situation brought up serious questions about Rose's work ethic. Despite missing Rose, the Bulls did win their first-round series against the favored Brooklyn Nets in seven hotly contested games. The Bulls were known for their strong defense and would need every bit of it to stop the high-powered Miami Heat attack.

Behind 27 points from tiny point guard Nate Robinson, the Chicago Bulls stunned the Heat in game one with a 93–86 upset win. Robinson also had 9 assists, and the Heat were totally caught off guard by the speedster. As usual, LeBron did his part with 24 points, 8 rebounds, and 7 assists, but with little extra help, it wasn't enough as the Bulls stole game one. Allen got hot in game two and scorched the Bulls stingy defense for 21 points. Backup point guard Norris Cole came off the bench to pull down 6 rebounds, the most of all Heat players. LeBron played the role of contributor and helped by dishing out 9 assists in the 115–78 blowout.

Game three was another bloodbath. Chicago resorted to playing extremely physically—and even down-right dirty at times—to compete with the Heat. It wasn't enough, and, despite Boozer scoring 21 points, the Heat were just far too much to handle. LeBron led the team with 25 points and 7 assists while Bosh pulled down a torrid 19 rebounds. the Bulls simply couldn't do anything to score without their best player and were held to 65 points in an 88–65 game four blowout loss. LeBron remained hot with a 27-point, 7-rebound, and 8-assist performance. A few nights later, the Heat wrapped it up with a 94–91 victory at home, returning to the Eastern Conference Finals for the third straight year.

Waiting for the Heat to arrive at the Eastern Conference Finals were the Indiana Pacers. This was the third playoff meeting for these two teams, with each team winning one of the previous playoff series. The Pacers had a grudge brewing against the Heat ever since they blew a 2–1 series lead the prior season. Many in the media felt that the Pacers got cocky when they were up 2–1 and lost focus. They were now out to prove that was far from the case, as they took the Heat to the limit in game one and actually held a lead in the final seconds in Miami. The game went into overtime, and it appeared that the Pacers were about to steal game one when LeBron hit the game-winning layup at the buzzer to seal the victory at 103–102. Indiana head coach Frank Vogel took serious criticism following the game for not having one of his best defenders, Roy Hibbert, in the game for the final seconds. LeBron had 30 points, along with 10 rebounds and 10 assists. It was his ninth career playoff triple-double, tying him with Wilt Chamberlain for fourth all-time, and 3 blocked shots. It was another dominant performance by the best athlete on the planet!

The game-one loss spoiled an outstanding effort by Indiana star Paul George, who was quickly rising to become one of the game's top stars. George had 27 points and several clutch shots in the loss, and he was starting to encounter the same problem LeBron had early in his Cleveland days by not having enough talent around him. But he got the help he needed in game two when his teammate Roy Hibbert went off for 29 points and grabbed 10 rebounds while George remained consistent with 6 vital assists. LeBron also played a great game, scoring 36 points with 8 rebounds, but it wasn't enough for the Heat to win and the Indiana Pacers tied the series with a 97–93 victory to even up at one game apiece.

The series then traveled to Indiana for game three where, despite 21 points by West and 17 rebounds by Hibbert, the Pacers lost by 18 points in front of their hometown fans. The Heat cruised to the 114–96 victory on the strength of 22 points from LeBron combined with 9 monster rebounds from Chris Anderson. The Pacers bounced back in game four to once again even up the series with a 99–92 win. Hibbert continued to play well and led the Pacers with 23 points and 12 rebounds. LeBron led the Heat with 24 points, but the series was tied and heading back to South Beach.

In game five, it was the Heat using a big 30–13 third quarter to put the Pacers away and win the game, 90–79. LeBron remained a scoring inferno, dropping 30 points on the Pacers' defense and bringing the Heat within one win of returning to the NBA Finals. It was do-or-die time for the Indiana Pacers in game six, and for the second straight season it was played in front of their hometown fans. The Pacers needed to come out strong and not let the weight of the situation get the best of them. They did just that and held a commanding 52–37 lead at halftime. George was in firm command and led the Pacers with 28 points. LeBron led a small comeback and finished with 29 points and 6 assists. In the end, it was the Indiana Pacers taking game six by a score of 91–77.

Game seven was shaping up to be an instant classic when the Pacers took control early at Miami and held a 21–19 lead after the first quarter. It was then that the wheels came off for Indiana and the Heat took over. Behind LeBron, the Heat outscored the Pacers 33–16 in the second quarter, en route to a blowout 99–76 series-clinching win. Known for bringing his best game in game seven, LeBron has averaged 34.4 points in the seventh game of the postseason throughout his career and currently holds the best point average in NBA history at this writing. True to his nature, LeBron finished with 32 points, and the Miami Heat were headed back to the NBA Finals for the third straight year.

If the Miami Heat's Big Three symbolized everything wrong with the NBA, then their opponent in the NBA Finals symbolized everything right. The NBA was quickly becoming a superstar league in which most teams revolved around one player doing most of the work and the others trying not to get in the way. Even superstar-caliber teams like the Los Angeles Lakers had suffered through issues such as those when Shaq and Kobe couldn't play together and forced a split. Sports in general, not just in basketball but most team sports, are seen as team sports in which everyone needs to work together to make things happen on both sides of the ball. The whole era of teams becoming "super teams" with a few players and a bunch of ring chasers was the exact opposite ideal of what the NBA had been built upon. Teams like the 1980s Celtics and Lakers and the 1990s Bulls failed to exist anymore, with the San Antonio Spurs as the lone exception— the ultimate homegrown talented team that everyone loved. They had won four NBA Championship titles since 1999 under head coach

Gregg Popovich. The era began in 1999 when the established veteran David Robinson combined with rising young star Tim Duncan to win the NBA Championship over the New York Knicks. Four years later, in 2003, the Spurs won again against the New Jersey Nets in Robinson's final season. The Spurs are one of those rare teams where the superstars never leave and spend their entire career on the same team. This was evident as they also won the NBA Championship again in 2005 against the Detroit Pistons and a fourth time against the LeBron James–led Cleveland Cavaliers in the 2007 NBA Finals. When that series ended, it was rumored that Duncan consoled LeBron by telling him not to worry about the defeat because they would meet again. Six years later, Duncan's words had come true—just not in the way anyone had envisioned them.

The Spurs were led by a tough-but-smart coach in Popovich, or, as most of his players called him, "Pop." He was a hard-nosed coach who preached team basketball and didn't like to converse much with the media because he wanted to keep the attention focused on his players and not himself. Popovich grew up with a Serbian father and Croatian mother and started playing basketball as a very young boy. He attended Merrillville High School and graduated in 1970 from the United States Air Force Academy where he played basketball all four years. He was so intelligent that at one point Popovich considered a career with the CIA.

Years later, Popovich returned to the Air Force Academy as an assistant coach in 1973 under head coach Hank Egan, a position he held for six years. In 1979, he was named the head coach of Pomona-Pitzer College's men's basketball team. Popovich coached for Pomona-Pitzer from 1979 to 1988, leading the team to its first outright title in 68 years. Eventually his love of the game and coaching took him to the NBA when, following the 1987–88 season, Popovich joined Larry Brown as the lead assistant coach for the San Antonio Spurs.

From 1988 to 1992, Popovich was the top assistant under Brown, and it was a great learning experience for him.

In 1994, Popovich became San Antonio's general manager and vice president of basketball operations. After the Spurs got out to a 3–15 start in the 1996–1997 season (with Robinson sidelined with a preseason back injury), Popovich fired then head coach Bob Hill and named himself head coach. The Spurs' disastrous season allowed them to win the first overall pick in the NBA lottery draft pick that year, which they used to draft Tim Duncan out of Wake Forest University. Duncan fit the mold of what Popovich excelled at coaching with and, when combined with veteran center Robinson, went on to form what would be known as the Twin Towers. For Popovich and Duncan, it was the start of a beautiful relationship—the Spurs won the NBA title in only their second year together.

As previously mentioned, the Robinson–Duncan duo would go on to win numerous championships, but they didn't do it alone. Teammate Tony Parker, though born in Belgium, was raised in France, where he spent most of his young life playing basketball. While most Europeans focus on soccer, Parker was torn because although he liked soccer, it was the play of Michael Jordan that enthralled him and eventually caused him to focus solely on basketball. After playing in the French amateur leagues for two seasons, Parker turned professional and signed with Paris Basket Racing in 1999.

In the summer of 2000, Parker was invited to the Nike Hoop Summit in Indianapolis. In a contest between the American and European All-Stars, Parker recorded 20 points, 7 assists, 4 rebounds, and 2 steals, which caught the eye of several NBA teams, including the San Antonio Spurs. After a couple of tryouts, the Spurs decided to select Parker 28th overall in the 2001 NBA draft. Parker became a starter early in his rookie season and made 77 regular-season appearances, averaging 9.2 points, 4.3 assists, and 2.6 rebounds in 29.4

minutes per game. Parker would grow to become a key part in the 2003, 2005, and 2007 NBA Finals runs, including being named the 2007 NBA Finals MVP.

To go along with Duncan and Parker was the former NBA Sixth Man of the Year Award winner, Manu Ginóbili. He was the first man off the bench and better than most starters around the league. Ginóbili was another foreign player who grew up idolizing Michael Jordan and had a stellar career since being drafted by the Spurs in 2002—another big part of three of the team's NBA Championship wins.

The fact that the top three players for San Antonio, Duncan, Parker, and Ginóbili, were all drafted by the Spurs and stayed there through thick and thin made the Spurs even more likable. Instead of a dream team built through free agency, the Spurs were homegrown heroes. In 2013, the Spurs came in as the second seed in the West and held the league's third-best overall record at 58–24. They swept the Los Angeles Lakers in the first round before getting pushed to six games in round two against Stephen Curry and the Golden State Warriors before beating them. The Spurs advanced to the NBA Finals by sweeping the Memphis Grizzlies in the Western Conference Championship Series. The Spurs were playing great and looked to be a dangerous opponent in the finals for the Heat.

The Heat had won both games they played against the Spurs during the regular season, 105–100 on November 29, 2012, and 88–86 on March 31, 2013. For the first game, however, Popovich sat out Duncan, Parker, Ginóbili, and Danny Green. The Spurs were at the end of a long road trip, and in order to ensure they had enough rest for the playoffs, Popovich chose to needed to preserve his star players, as the team had some of the most veteran players in the league. Despite the absence of their four starters, the Spurs led the game until the final minute, when the Heat came back to win 105–100. In a bit of gamesmanship, the Heat pulled the same trick when they came to

San Antonio later in the season but LeBron, Wade, and Chalmers sat out with minor injuries. The Heat had clinched the playoffs at that point and didn't want show too many more of their cards, because they expected a possible matchup with the Spurs in the Finals.

When the Finals began with game one on June 6, 2013, people expected a good series, but few could predict the showdown that was about to unfold. The series marked the fifth time the Spurs had made it to the NBA Finals since 1999, second-most for any franchise in that span of time just behind the Los Angeles Lakers, who had played in six. The Spurs had won all of their previous four finals' appearances, but this series was the first time San Antonio would play in the finals without homecourt advantage. The series was also loaded with four former NBA Finals MVPs: Duncan and Parker for the Spurs and LeBron and Wade for the Heat.

Game one in Miami was an instant classic. It came down to the final seconds, and the Spurs were able to put the Heat away with Parker running a jump shot that banked off the backboard and went in with 5.2 seconds left to seal the victory. The Heat had been leading by 3 points entering the fourth quarter, but the Spurs closed them out strong in the fourth, outscoring the Heat 23–16 for the win. Parker led the Spurs with 21 points and 6 assists. LeBron did everything he could, compiling another triple-double with 18 points, 18 rebounds, and 10 assists. Wade scored 17 points heading into the fourth, but then he disappeared when it counted the most: He had no points in the final quarter. Bosh also faded down the stretch, scoring only 2 points in that last quarter.

Game two belonged to the Heat, who blew out the Spurs 103–84. The Spurs were playing the Heat tough until the middle of the third quarter, when the Heat caught fire and went on a 33–5 run to pull away and take a huge lead. The key to Miami's victory was that LeBron finally received substantial help. The Heat made 10 out of

19 three-point shots, and five players had double-digit scoring games—it was a total team effort.

The series arrived in San Antonio for game three where the Spurs were set to explode from beyond the three-point arc. San Antonio set the finals' record for the most three-pointers in a game of 16 and gave the Heat their worst loss in the franchise's playoff history. Green went wild from the three-point arc and scored 27 points to lead the Spurs. Little-known Gary Neal played one of the best games of his career, making 6 three-point shots and finishing with 24 total points. The game wasn't all highlights for San Antonio, though: Tony Parker scored just 6 points before he had to leave the game due to a hamstring injury. Even more shocking than the three-point explosion was that LeBron was held to just 7 of 21 shooting from the field, finishing with only 15 points, and did not shoot a single free throw for the first time in his Miami playoff career.

The Spurs failed to capitalize on the big victory and got blown out in game four at home, 109–93. The score was actually tied at halftime at 49 before Miami broke down the defense wall of San Antonio in the second half. LeBron led the Heat with 33 points, while Wade had 32 and Bosh 20. A big reason for the second-half decline was the fact that Parker completely disappeared and couldn't produce any points. Not only was the Heat's 16-point win their 12th double-figure victory in the 2013 postseason, it gave them the most double-digit wins of any team during a single postseason in NBA history. (The previous record was 11, held by five different teams, each winning the NBA Championship that postseason.)

Game five saw each team's Big Three begin to shine in their entirety for the first time in the series. Parker led the Spurs with 26 points, while Green scored 24 with 6 three-pointers, breaking the all-time record for three-pointers in a finals series previously set by Ray Allen in 2008. The biggest run of the game was 19–1 by San Antonio.

The Heat did everything they could to try and keep pace as LeBron and Wade turned in strong performances, leading the Heat with 25 points each while Allen had 5 three-pointers and scored 21 points total. Bosh also did his part by pulling down 11 rebounds, but it wasn't enough for the Heat, and the Spurs regained control of the series with a 114–104 win. The Spurs were headed back to South Beach with two chances to win the NBA Championship for a fifth time.

Game six of the 2013 NBA Finals is one that will be talked about for many years to come. It had more drama than 10 Hollywood movie scripts combined. This game is still considered by players and commentators to be one of the greatest games in NBA history. NBA legend Magic Johnson called it "one of the best two or three games" he had ever seen. So enthralling was the contest that it actually won a 2013 ESPY Award for Best Game!

The Spurs held a commanding 10-point lead heading into the fourth quarter. Most believed that a team with the veteran talent of San Antonio would not blow a 10-point lead on the road in a closeout game for the NBA Championship. However, most people wouldn't bet against LeBron either, and that's what made this game so exciting. The Heat used a triple-double performance from LeBron, who scored 32 points along with 11 assists and 10 rebounds, becoming the first player since Magic Johnson in 1991 to achieve two triple-doubles in the same NBA Finals series. The Heat also used 20 points from Mario Chalmers to cut into the lead.

LeBron led a 20–7 run for the Heat to start the fourth quarter, scoring 11 of the 20 points. With 2 minutes and 9 seconds remaining, the Heat pulled ahead 89–86, but then the Spurs went on a run of their own led by Parker, who shot a step-back three-pointer and a reverse layup in consecutive possessions to put the Spurs in the lead, 91–89.

Despite four league MVP awards and being widely regarded as the best player on the planet, LeBron started to fall away under the pressure. On the next possession, LeBron lost the ball in the post, which eventually led to a pair of Ginóbili free throws after an intentional foul by Allen on the other end, pushing the score to 93–89. LeBron then committed a second crucial turnover, forcing the ball into the hands of Ginóbili. The only hope for the Heat would be if the Spurs started to miss foul shots, and that was exactly what happened, as Ginóbili, who was fouled by Allen, would miss one of two free throws.

The Miami fans, who were not nearly as loyal as the Spurs fans that night, left the building in mass droves, thinking the game was over. They demonstrated little to no faith in their team. The camera crew showed thousands of people leaving the building in their white shirts, angry over what they perceived as the Heat losing the series.

With 28 seconds remaining, the Spurs were up 94–89, and league officials began bringing out the yellow tape to rope off the floor for the Larry O'Brien Trophy presentation. It was a bad omen, as players in both huddles saw the NBA officials taping off an area for the post-game celebration. Breaking out of the time-out, the Heat called a play for LeBron to shoot a three in which he promptly missed. Miller then tipped the rebound back to LeBron, who then converted on his second attempt and cut the lead to 2 points with 20 seconds remaining. The Heat immediately fouled Kawhi Leonard on the next inbound pass in their failed attempt to steal the ball. Leonard missed one of the two foul shots, keeping the lead at only 3 points and leaving the door open just a crack for the Heat to make one last comeback. The missed foul shot would haunt Leonard for an entire year before he would get the chance to make up for it in a very gigantic way.

Coming out of the time-out, everyone in the nation knew the ball would be going to LeBron. Everything was on the line for the Heat, and if they couldn't make a three-pointer, the series and the season would be over and everyone would be talking about another underachieving Miami Heat season. It almost happened: LeBron missed a

26-foot jumper from beyond the arc, but Bosh was able to collect the desperation offensive rebound before passing to Allen, who calmly stepped backward and made a three-point basket from the right corner to send the game into overtime. It was the exact reason the Heat had worked so hard to sign Allen in the off-season. Allen had bailed out LeBron and given the Heat new life. He had made many big shots in his career, but this was by far his biggest.

The scene was almost comedic as the cameras cut to outside the arena showing dozens of Miami Heat fans racing to get back in the game, only to be turned away. Some in the media referred to this as the "Headband Game," as LeBron got his trademark headband knocked off early in the fourth quarter and never put it back on. Regardless of that, no one can dispute this was a classic game headed for overtime. A small bit of criticism was given to Popovich, who opted to go with a small lineup to defend the perimeter in the closing moments of the fourth quarter, resulting in Duncan being on the bench as both of the Heat's three-pointers came off of rebounds. Some in the media feel that if Duncan had still been in the game, he could have pulled down one of the missed shots and closed out the game at the foul line. Even four-time NBA Championship winning coaches like Popovich get second-guessed every now and then. Duncan had 30 points and 17 rebounds, but there wasn't much he could do from the bench. The Heat's 103–100 overtime win improved their all-time postseason overtime record to 8–1, a 0.889 postseason winning percentage, which is currently the best record held among teams with at least three overtime games played and the second-highest percentage among all teams.

Kenny Roda shared his memories of that wild night, detailing the following:

> *I remember the NBA officials coming out and roping off the court, getting ready for a Spurs celebration. They were up by 5 with a few seconds left, and I remember Gregg Popovich having Tim Duncan*

on the bench, which hurt them because both three-pointers were off of rebounds. It was the inability of the Spurs to get rebounds that the series was then lost. I think Gregg Popovich realized it as a coach that his decision let the team down late in game six. For me, San Antonio lost that series more than the Heat won that series. Five points, you're the Spurs, there is no way you should lose that game. Somehow, some way, they found a way to give it away to the Miami Heat.

The Heat dominated the overtime period, getting a burst of energy and using the momentum of the comeback to jump out to a lead and hold onto it until the closing seconds of overtime in front of a half-empty Miami crowd. Green did have one last chance to tie the game for the Spurs in the closing seconds with a three-pointer, but it was blocked by Bosh, and the Heat won the game 103–100. Though that block was clearly a foul committed by Bosh, in that situation—in Miami in overtime—there was no way referee Joe Crawford was calling it.

If anyone ever had any doubt about the greatness and killer instinct of LeBron James, all they would have to do is watch a tape of game seven of the 2013 NBA Finals and all doubts would be answered. Moving into game seven of this series, LeBron scored 37 points, including five 5 three-pointers, and grabbed 12 rebounds to lead Miami to a 95–88 victory and their second consecutive NBA Championship. It was also a big night for Shane Battier, who scored 18 points on 6 three-pointers to offset a scoreless night by both Bosh and Allen.

Parker and Ginóbili both played horribly in game seven, and the Heat took full advantage. The Spurs trailed by just 2 points with 50 seconds remaining in the game. They had a chance to tie the game, but Duncan, who was guarded by Battier, missed a shot under the basket and a follow-up tip-in attempt. LeBron went on to hit a 17-foot jumper on the following possession that secured the victory. He tied

Tommy Heinsohn's record set in 1957 for most points in an NBA Finals game seven win, and he won his second straight NBA Finals MVP. The Heat became the fourth team to win an NBA title by coming back from a 3–2 series deficit and winning the final two games at home. LeBron had finally reached redemption from his 2007 NBA Finals loss to the Spurs, roughly a little over a year later, and he would once again find redemption of a much different kind.

The TV ratings for this epic series were through the roof. Game six garnered a 12.3 Nielsen rating and was viewed by more than 20 million households. It was an incredible rating, but it was beaten by game seven, which drew a 15.3 rating and was viewed by 26 million households. Anyone in search of further proof that LeBron James is the greatest player in the game today needs only to review the accomplishments listed below.

LeBron scored 32 points in game six of the 2013 NBA Finals and then made 37 points in game seven. He became the first player in NBA history to score consecutive 30-point games to help rally his team from a 3–2 series deficit to win an NBA title. LeBron finished the 2013 postseason by recording his fourth straight 30-point game seven that fateful night. He had previously scored 32 points versus the Pacers on June 3, 2013; 31 points versus the Celtics on June 9, 2012; and 45 points versus the Celtics on May 18, 2008. He has also tied the record of the only other player to score at least 30 points in four consecutive game sevens held by Wilt Chamberlain. LeBron's 18 points, 18 rebounds, and 10 assists versus San Antonio on June 6, 2013, marked the 28th time he led his team outright (no ties) in each of those categories during the playoffs—the most in NBA postseason history. In addition, LeBron has been the outright game-high leader, with no ties in each of those categories eight times, and also the most in NBA postseason history. His eight such games are more than the combined total of the next three players to achieve this feat.

But despite these incredible records and accomplishments, once again the only title that meant anything to LeBron was "champion."

As LeBron and his teammates basked in the glow of another NBA Championship, the Heat began to prepare for another defense of their title and looked to three-peat as champions. Management decided to cut Mike Miller in the off-season, though it was not a popular move with LeBron, who had developed a friendship with Miller since coming to the Heat. It was simply a business move as the Heat simply couldn't afford to pay Miller while carrying so many high-dollar contracts. The Heat did take a risk and sign former number-one overall draft pick Greg Oden, who was often injured since coming into the league in the fall of 2007 from Ohio State.

Oden led Lawrence North High School in Indianapolis, Indiana, to three consecutive Indiana Class 4A Basketball Championships before graduating in 2006. He was named *Parade*'s High School Co-Player of the Year and the National Boys Basketball Player of the Year, both in 2005. Oden was also named Indiana's "Mr. Basketball" in 2006. There was a lot of hype surrounding him as he enrolled at Ohio State University for the 2006–07 season. But the often-injured Oden once again ran into a minor roadblock, undergoing surgery on his right wrist in June 2006 to repair a ligament injury that had occurred late in his senior high school season. The injury pushed back his debut with the Buckeyes to December 2, 2006. Oden was later named to the First Team All-Big Ten, as well being voted the conference's Defensive Player of the Year for 2006. Oden went on to lead the Ohio State Buckeyes to the National Championship game that following March. In the title game, Oden scored 25 points with 12 rebounds and 4 blocked shots in a losing effort against the Florida Gators.

It was the last college game for Oden, who would leave college that spring and declare himself eligible for the 2007 NBA draft, where he was selected first overall by the Portland Trail Blazers. The

Trail Blazers passed on Kevin Durant, certainly a decision they would grow to regret: On September 14, 2007, Oden would undergo microfracture surgery on his injured right knee, causing him to miss his entire rookie season.

Oden returned to the floor in 2008–09 with the Trailblazers and played in 61 games, starting 39 of them. He looked decent when he was healthy enough to stay on the court, averaging 8.9 points with 7 rebounds a game—okay numbers, but not nearly the kind expected out of an overall number-one pick. He battled injuries again in 2009–2010, playing just 21 games and getting subpar numbers. Oden's knees were never healthy enough to keep him on the court for any considerable amount of time, and from 2012 to 2013, he was out of basketball altogether because no one was willing to take a chance on him. The Heat, however, took that chance and brought Oden in for the start of the 2013–14 season. He was the team's only addition of any name value. They still had everyone else in play from the previous season and looked to make another strong run at the title.

The one point of worry for the Heat was their aging roster. They had nine players in their 10th year or longer, players who would need plenty of rest to get ready for the latest playoff push. It was a major factor that Coach Spoelstra had to contend with all season long. Because of Dwayne Wade's aging knees, he would start only 53 games that season. It was the first sign of many that this would be the end of the Miami's Big Three.

The 2013–14 season started off well for Miami with a solid win over their old foes, the Chicago Bulls, who lost to the Heat 107–95. Miami began a road trip the next night with a loss to the Philadelphia 76ers, who would go on to have the worst record in the league that season. The following game wasn't much better—the Heat lost to the Brooklyn Nets, something that they would do three more times that season as the Nets swept the season series. The Heat managed to bounce back to win their next 12 out of 13 games, complete with an impressive 10-game winning streak. The team remained hot, and after beating the Los Angeles Lakers 101–95, the Heat's record improved to 22–6.

Miami remained consistent and would routinely win four out of every five games they played. They ripped off another 8-game winning streak in mid- to late February. It was during that month that LeBron returned to the All-Star Game and played with that game's MVP, Kyrie Irving. It was after that game that the rumors began of a possible Irving–LeBron combo some day, as their chemistry was great.

On March 3, 2014, LeBron had a career-high 61 points against the Charlotte Bobcats. His 61 points were also a franchise high, breaking Glen Rice's previously held record. At that time, the win moved the Heat to a 43–14 record. They were in a battle with the red-hot Indiana Pacers for the number-one spot in the Eastern Conference. It was after that big night by LeBron that the Heat hit their first stumbling block of the season. They proceeded to lose five of their next six games, including losses to teams such as San Antonio, Houston, Chicago, Brooklyn, and Denver—all playoff-caliber teams. The Heat bounced back with a 113–104 win over the powerful Houston Rockets at home. It was then that LeBron was to make one last trip home to Cleveland.

On Tuesday, March 18, 2014, LeBron returned to Cleveland as a member of the visiting team. Many Clevelanders secretly hoped that this would be the last time they would have to bear this pain, as they prayed that LeBron would come home, and most fans actually cheered him throughout the game. It was a far cry from his first trip home on December 2, 2010, when the entire crowd booed him loudly every time he touched the ball.

The game was a barn burner. LeBron brought everything he had to the court and seemed inspired by the sudden cheers he was hearing from the crowd. LeBron took no prisoners and scored 43 points while pulling down 6 rebounds and dishing out 4 assists. He knew he would have to play well, because it was one of the 29 games that season that Wade did not play in.

The Miami Heat used the hot start by LeBron to get off to one of their own, leading the Cavaliers 37–25. Cleveland was determined not to get blown out again and fought back in the second quarter, outscoring the Heat 29–22 and climbing back in the game to only trail by 5 points heading into halftime. The Cavaliers kept pushing and doing their best to stay with the Heat, managing to force a tie game heading into the fourth quarter. LeBron and the rest of the Heat managed to hold on to the lead and beat the Cavaliers one more time, 100–96. The Heat had faced the Cavaliers 16 times since LeBron had left in 2010 and went 15–1 in those games.

The Heat struggled again after leaving Cleveland with the victory, losing six of their last eight games and failing to reclaim the number-one seed in the Eastern Conference. Instead, they would have to play as the number-two seed, having finished with a 54–28 record—two wins shy of first-place Indiana.

Michael Jordan, who was LeBron's childhood hero and one of the Hall of Famers who was critical of LeBron for leaving Cleveland, was also the owner of the Charlotte Bobcats, the first-round opponent for the Miami Heat in the 2014 NBA Playoffs. LeBron took it upon himself to put on a clinic in front of his idol, and the Heat blasted the Bobcats in four straight games to sweep them right out of the playoffs. In a game-one 99–88 win, LeBron scored 27 points with 9 rebounds. Game two wasn't much different, with the Heat winning 101–97 in a tight match that saw LeBron unload 32 points, 6 rebounds, 8 assists, and an amazing 4 steals. LeBron remained on fire in game three with a 98–85 win for the Heat, scoring 30 points and pulling off 10 rebounds and 2 steals. It was clear that as long as LeBron was playing at this level, no one could stop him. The Heat completed their sweep with a game-four 109–98 drubbing of the Bobcats. It was another near triple-double for LeBron, who scored 31 points with 9 assists, 7 rebounds, and 3 steals. It was one of the most dominating playoff series by a single player in NBA history.

The second-round matchup, against the Brooklyn Nets, was supposed to be the true test for Miami. The Heat had lost four times to the Nets during the season, and some thought they had the Heat's number. The Nets were stacked with talent, having traded away their future to Boston for Paul Pierce and Kevin Garnett to play with Joe Johnson, and their Russian billionaire owner, Mikhail Prokhorov, spared no expense to bring in the very best and also take some chances on big names. Prokhorov brought in troubled former player Jason Kidd to coach his personal dream team; unfortunately, Kidd caused problems for his coaching staff right away—he found himself suspended for the team's first two regular-season games due to a highly publicized drunk-driving incident in the summer of 2012.

The Nets' season began on October 30, 2013, with a 94–98 loss to the Cleveland Cavaliers, and they got off to a pretty slow start after that. Despite the embarrassing antics of their head coach, the Nets managed to finally turn things around and finish sixth in the Eastern Conference. They squeaked by the Toronto Raptors in a thrilling seven-game series in round one and looked forward to the matchup with the Heat.

The Miami Heat came into the series angry, because many actually doubted the three-time defending champions as they prepared to square off against the Nets. LeBron knew that once again he would have to take matters into his own hands and lead a dismantling of the Nets. Game one was a 107–86 blowout win for the Heat. Allen had a big game for the Heat as well, with 19 points off the bench. The Heat won easily in game two with a 94–82 defeat of the Nets. There was a lot of talk that Pierce and Garnett wanted revenge on the Heat for knocking them out of the playoffs the previous two years with the Boston Celtics, but they sure weren't playing like it in the first two games.

The Nets managed to sneak in a game-three 104–90 win—LeBron had 28 points in the contest but got little help elsewhere. It was the first playoff loss for the Heat in their last eight playoff games. LeBron had enough messing around with the Nets and put the Heat on his shoulders in game four, exploded for 49 points in the 102–96 win to take a commanding 3–1 series lead. Game five was much closer but ended in the same result, with a 96–94 nail-biting win for the Heat. LeBron scored 29 more points and put the finishing touches on a 4–1 series victory.

The Heat were set for an Eastern Conference Championship rematch with the Indiana Pacers. It was the only common factor from the prior season, because this was far from being an ordinary playoff series. The first 11 days of the playoffs saw at least one road team win on their opponent's home floor. The 24 road wins is an NBA Playoffs record in the first round. In addition, the 2014 NBA Playoffs also featured a record eight first-round games that went into overtime, including four straight games between the Memphis Grizzlies and the Oklahoma City Thunder. Five of the eight first-round series were extended to seven games, which tied the record for the most number of game sevens in the history of NBA Playoffs. All three teams from Texas made the playoffs for the first time since 2009. Also, for the first time since 2005, the Los Angeles Lakers and New York Knicks did not qualify for the playoffs in the same year, and for the first time since 1994, the Lakers and Celtics missed the playoffs in the same season. Furthermore, this was the first time in NBA history that the Knicks, Celtics, and Lakers missed the playoffs in the same year. While each team seemed to be going through a war to get to the next round, Miami was cruising along, winning eight of nine games and getting plenty of rest.

The Indiana Pacers, who finished the season with a conference-best 56 wins, had suddenly turned into a dramatic train wreck. A late-season trade of Danny Granger for Evan Turner seemed to throw everything off for the Pacers. Frank Vogel had lost control of his locker room, and players like Roy Hibbert were barely trying, walking up and down the court and pouting on the bench. The Pacers had worked hard all season to almost throw it all away in the playoffs. They snuck by the low-seeded Atlanta Hawks in the first round in seven games before just getting by the Washington Wizards in the second round. To get past the Heat, the Pacers were going to need to get it together quickly.

This series marked the third consecutive year that the Heat and the Pacers faced off in the playoffs, including the second consecutive time in the Conference Finals. Indiana sensed the urgency in game one and jumped to a 10-point lead early and never looked back, leading by as much as 19. Wade looked like the player of old, scoring 27 points, but it wasn't nearly enough—the Pacers took game one 107–96. The Heat responded by taking game two, 87–83, and in the process claimed the homecourt advantage. LeBron and Wade led the Heat when it mattered most and scored the Heat's last 20 points. The Pacers were up late, but star player Paul George dove for a loose ball when Wade kneed him in the head. This gave George a concussion, and he was never the same player for the rest of the series. It also didn't help matters for the Pacers that David West was also poked in the eye and couldn't return to the game.

Game three in Miami was a wild affair. The Pacers started strong, leading by as much as 15 in the second quarter before the Heat cut the lead to 4 points by halftime. The Heat would eventually pull away in the fourth quarter with the help of Allen's 16 points, including

4 three-pointers in the fourth quarter alone. Despite how hard the Pacers claimed to be playing, the Heat were having their way with them. LeBron led all scorers once again, with 27 clutch points. Game four wasn't too much different, as LeBron yet again led the Heat with 32 points to give them a 102–90 victory. The Pacers never held a single lead in game four and were fading fast.

In game five back in Indiana, the Heat led by 11 by the third quarter. However, LeBron received his fourth and fifth fouls early in the third, putting him on the bench and giving the Pacers momentum to mount a comeback. George led the Pacers with 37 points, including 21 in the fourth quarter alone. LeBron had his worst playoff game of the series that night, scoring just 7 points after being plagued by foul trouble all game long. The Heat actually had a chance to win and were down by 2 points with a few seconds remaining. LeBron drove the lane and kicked it out to an open Bosh for a three-point attempt that clanked off the rim. The Pacers hung on to win 93–90, sending the series back to Miami for game six, where the Heat blew the doors off the Pacers in a 117–92 win. LeBron and Bosh both had 25 points, and the Heat would return to the NBA Finals for the fourth straight season.

Heading into the 2014 NBA Finals, LeBron had done everything a basketball player could possibly do: He had accumulated considerable wealth and fame as a result of numerous endorsement deals; had been ranked as one of America's most influential and popular athletes; had been featured in books, documentaries, and television commercials and had even hosted the ESPY Awards and Saturday Night Live; was a two-time NBA National Champion, a two-time NBA Finals MVP, a four-time League MVP, a 10-time All-Star, a two-time NBA All-Star Game MVP, a 10-time All NBA Team selection, a six-time

All-Defensive Team selection, the 2008 NBA Scoring Champion, and the 2004 NBA Rookie of the Year; and was a two-time gold medal winner and one-time bronze medal winner in the Olympics playing for Team USA. Even with all of these accomplishments, however, it was the next 30 days that would define the next 30 years of his legacy.

The fans welcome LeBron James back to Cleveland.   Photo: kennyroda.com

CHAPTER TEN

Redemption

The 2014 NBA Finals would see the Miami Heat once more doing battle with the San Antonio Spurs. This was a repeat of the previous year's finals, in which Miami won in seven games, handing the Spurs the franchise's first-ever Finals defeat. This also marked the 12th Finals rematch for the two teams.

This was the Miami Heat's fourth straight appearance in the NBA Finals—they would be the first team since the 1987 Boston Celtics to make it to four straight NBA Finals, and only the fourth team in NBA history to do so to date.

The Spurs held the homecourt advantage, having finished the regular season with the best record in the NBA. They ran a ball movement–style offense and a very deep bench, with no player averaging more than 30 minutes during the regular season. This was the San Antonio Spurs' sixth appearance in the NBA Finals, their only loss coming in the prior season against the Heat.

The Spurs had been up by 5 points with less than 30 seconds to go in a possible clincher in game six of the previous season, and they had to cope with that loss all year. The Spurs were out for revenge and were prepared to use their entire roster to win. Small forward Kawhi Leonard didn't forget having missed the foul shot that kept the lead at 3 points for Miami in game six, leaving the door open just wide enough for Ray Allen to send it into overtime with a game-tying three-pointer. Leonard hadn't forgotten about the pain of losing that game and then the series, but it would be the pain of the previous year's disappointment that would ignite Leonard in the most memorable way in this series.

Game one of the series began on June 5, 2014, in San Antonio. Call it fate for the Spurs or just plain bad luck for the Heat, but the air-conditioning unit broke that night at the AT&T Center. The temperature on the floor reached almost 90 degrees at certain points. At first the Heat didn't seemed fazed by the warm temperature and led most of the game. They held a slim lead a few minutes into the fourth quarter when the conditions caused LeBron to dehydrate and suffer cramps, limiting him to just 5 minutes of playing time in the fourth quarter. With LeBron out of the game, the Spurs went on a 15–4 run and outscored the Heat 36–17 in the fourth quarter. The Spurs had looked sluggish all game and had several costly turnovers, but the moment LeBron left the game they were given new life and exploded, draining shots every time they touched the ball. The Spurs couldn't miss and the Heat couldn't score without LeBron. It was a perfect time for Bosh and Wade to step up, but they simply didn't. Instead, without LeBron in the lineup, the Heat crumbled and allowed the Spurs to walk away with a 110–95 win. LeBron once again had done everything he could, but the cramps were just too much and Coach Spoelstra would not allow him to play through the pain.

LeBron and the air conditioner both returned to working form for game two, as LeBron scored 35 points and pulled down 10 rebounds, leading the Heat to a 98–96 win. It was after this game that Gregg Popovich pulled Leonard aside and told him he needed to step up his coverage of LeBron and produce more offensively. Leonard heard his coach loud and clear.

Leonard was a standout college player at San Diego State. In his freshman year with the Aztecs, he led the team to a 25–9 record and the Mountain West Conference tournament title. Leonard led the MWC in rebounding, was named MWC Freshman of the Year, First Team All-MWC, and was the 2010 MWC Tournament MVP. During his sophomore season, Leonard averaged 15.7 points and 10.4 rebounds as the Aztecs finished with a 34–3 record. He helped them win the conference tournament championship that year as well. Leonard was named to the Second Team All-America and would forgo his final two seasons at San Diego State to enter the 2011 NBA draft. Leonard was selected with the 15th overall pick in the draft that year by the Indiana Pacers, but he was later traded on draft night to the San Antonio Spurs along with Erazem Lorbek and Dāvis Bertāns in exchange for George Hill. Leonard placed fourth in Rookie of the Year voting and was named to the 2012 All-Rookie First Team. His career was off to a solid start but was haunted by that one missed foul shot.

In game three, Leonard put to rest any memory of the missed foul shot when he went off for a career-high 29 points. The Spurs were on fire from the start and couldn't miss a shot; it was a finals-record 75.8 percent shooting effort from the team during the first half. Leonard made his first six shots and was 10 of 13 for the game. San Antonio led by as many as 25 points and held a dominating 71–50 halftime lead. Behind a remarkable effort by LeBron, the Heat actually fought back in the third quarter to cut the lead to 81–74 at one point, but never got any closer. The Spurs got hot once again and the final score was 111–92. The Heat, who had been 8–0 at home in the playoffs, were led by LeBron and Wade with 22 points apiece. Another key decision by Coach Popovich was to insert Boris Diaw into the starting lineup to create more ball movement.

Game four was more of the same: Leonard scored 20 points and made 14 rebounds in another rout of the Heat. The Spurs won 107–86 to take a 3–1 lead in the series. It was the first time in 13 prior playoff losses for the Heat that they didn't respond with a win. The last time the Heat lost two games in a row in a playoff series was in the 2012 Eastern Conference Finals against Boston. The Spurs defense held Miami to just 35 percent shooting in the first half. A backbreaking moment was a dunk by Leonard, followed by a missed foul shot that none of the Heat players went for. LeBron mounted another stellar effort, with 28 points and 8 rebounds, but it simply wasn't enough, as both Wade and Bosh were nowhere to be found.

Much like the previous three wins for the Spurs, game five was another blowout for them with a 104–87 series-clinching victory. Leonard put on a show with 22 points and 10 rebounds. Later he would be named the series MVP. LeBron did everything he could to try to will the Heat to a victory, including an incredible 17-point first-quarter performance as the Heat built a 22–6 lead. As usual, LeBron lacked the needed help around him, and the Spurs mounted a 37–13 run from the beginning of the second quarter through the middle of the third to take a commanding lead. LeBron finished with 31 points and 10 rebounds in only 41 minutes, but he sat out the last half of the final quarter. As he sat there, the frustration showed on his face, and one could almost sense a major change coming. For the first time in a long time, people started to believe that a return to Cleveland was no longer a long shot.

One major factor to consider was how a move by LeBron back to Cleveland would affect his brand. Ken Carman explained why he thought it was important for LeBron to stay in a positive light and considered some of the challenges he would face:

LeBron James is going on 30 years old and going on the second half of his career. He is on the back nine of his career, so to speak. That is where some of the trust in his players really comes into play. LeBron very much wants to become a brand and very much so wants to become an icon. Well, if you're going to become that, then people need to trust you because people need to trust brands. You need to be able to trust what you're buying. I really think a move back to Cleveland would be his final move because the Cavs are going to bend over backwards to do everything they need to do for him. And now he is smack dab in the middle of his backyard and he has proven himself. I think that it entices other players to come in for a little bit less and you can have that salary cap open up. I do think the biggest difference between then and now really is trust.

As the Heat were drowning in the finals, the San Antonio Spurs were putting the finishing touches on a 4–1 series win. The Spurs won big to close the series, averaging a point differential in the NBA Finals of 18 points per victory—the largest differential in NBA Finals history—and LeBron didn't even play the last 6 minutes of the series clincher. You could sense it in the air: The fate of the Heat, and the NBA, was about to change greatly.

Later, when asked in the postseries press conference about his plans for the off-season and whether he would opt out of his contract early, LeBron was very noncommittal and simply stated that he needed time to spend with his family. He wasn't tipping his cards, although the majority of the national news felt strongly that the chances of LeBron staying in Miami were almost guaranteed.

As the off-season frenzy began, that hunch remained strong. What the national media couldn't control was the fairy tale that began to take shape. LeBron's wife, Savannah James, was the first to hint that a possible return was in the works when she sent out a message on her Instagram account attached to a picture of Ohio with a heart on Akron that read, "Home Sweet Home, the countdown is real!" A return to Cleveland continued to look more and more possible when LeBron opted out of his contract with Miami days before he had to make his decision. This didn't mean that his days in Miami were done just yet; it did mean that now LeBron could sign with any team he wanted.

The longer LeBron went without re-signing with the Heat, the more and more people started to believe that maybe Cleveland actually was in the game once for retaining the services of "King James." The hysteria hit an all-time high on Sunday evening, July 6, 2014, when Dan Gilbert's private jet was spotted flying to South Beach. The rumor mill ran rampant with speculation that Gilbert was there to talk LeBron into coming back home. At first the rumor was denied, but later it would turn out to be true. In an interview with Yahoo Sports' Adrian Wojnarowski on July 11, 2014, Gilbert described the exact scenario of the meeting and why it was so important to apologize and clear the air with LeBron over the letter he had published in 2010. Gilbert explained, "We had five great years together and one terrible night. I told him how sorry I was, expressed regret for how that night went and how I let all the emotion and passion for the situation carry me away. I told him I wish I had never done it, that I wish I could take it back."

It took a lot of guts and humility from Gilbert to admit that he had reacted too harshly and too quickly in the heat of the moment. LeBron told Gilbert that he himself had wished he had handled things differently, and that they both made mistakes they needed to move on from. LeBron, it seemed, was angry with himself for how he had handled his decision to leave Cleveland. It was a breakthrough moment for LeBron and Gilbert, and for the first time in four years, peace was on its way to being achieved. Even if LeBron never came back to Cleveland, it was a moment that needed to happen. Both men needed to clear the air for the ease of their own consciences. Gilbert left that day with no deal in place, but for LeBron and himself, they did something more important than dollars and contracts—they both cleared the heavy weight from their shoulders and in their hearts. No matter what happened next, it was a healing both men needed.

Gilbert went on to tell Wojnarowski in that same interview:

Do a Google search on me, and it's the first thing that comes up. To a certain segment of society, it's like somebody killed somebody, like somebody killed their kid. I told LeBron, "That letter didn't hurt anybody more than it hurt me." For the first two months, I kept thousands of letters—not hundreds—thousands written to me. There were 90-year-old ladies and CEOs, and I realized that that letter had transcended the event, went far beyond LeBron. After a few months, I would reread it and just be full of regret. That wasn't me, that wasn't who I am. I didn't mean most of the things I said in there. The venom it produced, from all sides, I wish . . . I wish I had never done it.

For Gilbert to come out and admit this showed true class and the fact that even a billionaire can admit a mistake. It is a lesson that all of America could learn from. The peace achieved between LeBron and Gilbert proves that no problem between two people is too big to be overcome. Two men with all the fame and money in the world, seeking forgiveness from each other in search of peace—it's a message that anyone can appreciate and emulate.

Twitter caught fire as local Cleveland basketball reporter Sam Amico picked up more than 25,000 extra followers in a matter of hours. Everybody was desperate for information. People started to hang on every tweet from anyone in the know. It got to the point that every sports radio show in Miami and Cleveland turned into 100 percent LeBron coverage. Everyone had a theory and a source, and the frenzy reached a level even greater than that of 2010.

Meanwhile, Chris Bosh was offered a four-year, $88 million deal with the Houston Rockets, but he refused to give them an answer because he wanted to see what his teammate and friend would do first. It was unprecedented to hear of an athlete putting that kind of money on hold because he was too hung up on what someone else was going to do.

Carmelo Anthony was being recruited heavily by both the New York Knicks and the Los Angeles Lakers, but even the hype behind Anthony paled in comparison to the insane amount of press and extremely personal coverage LeBron was getting. It got to the point that every single move LeBron made was being reported on Twitter. The hype was real, the pulse of Cleveland was raging, and the fans stayed up all night in anticipation of an announcement coming at any second. Even media personalities such as Chris Broussard, Chris Sheridan, and Steve Silas started to believe and report that Cleveland was a serious contender.

The Cavaliers continued to apply the pressure and show LeBron that they were for real when they pulled off a trade with the Nets and Celtics that cleared up more than $20 million in cap room. Cleveland dealt Tyler Zeller, Jarrett Jack, and Sergey Karasev as part of the move. The cap room was made to bring in LeBron and have the means to sign him to a max contract. Although he never gave Gilbert any promise he was coming back, this was a bold move by Gilbert to show LeBron that Cleveland was a serious contender.

Sensing that his dream team was slipping away, Pat Riley called an emergency meeting in Las Vegas at LeBron's camp on Wednesday, July 9, 2014, to discuss re-signing LeBron with the Heat. Riley pitched LeBron hard on the idea that, despite only having two returning players on the roster, the Heat had the funds available to bring him back with a max contract and still be able to sign both Bosh and Wade for smaller deals, giving the team access to bring in other talent around him. Riley had picked up Danny Granger and Josh McRoberts in free agency already, had planned on signing Bosh and Wade, and had already drafted LeBron's favorite college point guard, Shabazz Napier, from the National Championship–winning University of Connecticut Huskies. This was crucial because LeBron had made it known during the NCAA tournament that he had a special liking for Napier, calling him the best player in the tournament. It was seen as a move strictly to appeal to LeBron; if he wasn't on the team, the Heat would have picked someone else.

Jerry Mires gave his thoughts on the odds of LeBron coming home to Cleveland at that time:

> *I'd say 25 percent of it goes to him wanting to come back home and at least 50 percent of it is because of his wife. He can't fix his stupid national legacy. Nobody will give him the respect that his statistics would seem to deserve because the blemish was the proof. LeBron screwed himself by leaving, and I get why he left, but all he had to do on the first day of free agency was inform the Cavs that he was not coming back and let them know they needed to move on without him while they still had time. He could have still done everything else the same, but he could have left Cleveland off the hook, which is what I think most people were upset about. For everyone who wants to paint this happy LeBron-goes-home fairytale, I guarantee you that if Wade was healthier and the salary cap in Miami wasn't messed up, this would have never even been discussed.*

Evening turned into night, and the decision still hadn't been made. LeBron had wrapped up his skills camp in Vegas and was headed back to Miami. He was spotted with Wade on his trip back, and many felt this may have been the kiss of death for Cleveland. It was later revealed that Wade still didn't know of LeBron's decision at that point. Everyone went to bed late Thursday night and awoke Friday morning still not knowing.

As the morning dragged into the early afternoon, it finally happened: LeBron James had made his decision, and the prodigal son was coming home! He made his announcement in an essay to *Sports Illustrated* reporter Lee Jenkins and posted it on SI.com. His emotional essay to the fans read as follows:

Before anyone ever cared where I would play basketball, I was a kid from Northeast Ohio. It's where I walked. It's where I ran. It's where I cried. It's where I bled. It holds a special place in my heart. People there have seen me grow up. I sometimes feel like I'm their son. Their passion can be overwhelming. But it drives me. I want to give them hope when I can. I want to inspire them when I can. My relationship with Northeast Ohio is bigger than basketball. I didn't realize that four years ago. I do now.

Remember when I was sitting up there at the Boys & Girls Club in 2010? I was thinking, "This is really tough." I could feel it. I was leaving something I had spent a long time creating. If I had to do it all over again, I'd obviously do things differently, but I'd still have left. Miami, for me, has been almost like college for other kids. These past four years helped raise me into who I am. I became a better player and a better man. I learned from a franchise that had been where I wanted to go. I will always think of Miami as my second home. Without the experiences I had there, I wouldn't be able to do what I'm doing today.

I went to Miami because of D-Wade and CB. We made sacrifices to keep UD. I loved becoming a big bro to Rio. I believed we could do something magical if we came together. And that's exactly what we did! The hardest thing to leave is what I built with those guys. I've talked to some of them and will talk to others. Nothing will ever change what we accomplished. We are brothers for life. I also want to thank Micky Arison and Pat Riley for giving me an amazing four years.

I'm doing this essay because I want an opportunity to explain myself uninterrupted. I don't want anyone thinking, "He and Erik Spoelstra didn't get along. . . . He and Riles didn't get along. . . . The Heat couldn't put the right team together." That's absolutely not true.

I'm not having a press conference or a party. After this, it's time to get to work.

When I left Cleveland, I was on a mission. I was seeking championships, and we won two. But Miami already knew that feeling. Our city hasn't had that feeling in a long, long, long time. My goal is still to win as many titles as possible, no question. But what's most important for me is bringing one trophy back to Northeast Ohio.

I always believed that I'd return to Cleveland and finish my career there. I just didn't know when. After the season, free agency wasn't even a thought. But I have two boys and my wife Savannah is pregnant with a girl. I started thinking about what it would be like to raise my family in my hometown. I looked at other teams, but I wasn't going to leave Miami for anywhere except Cleveland. The more time passed, the more it felt right. This is what makes me happy.

To make the move I needed the support of my wife and my mom, who can be very tough. The letter from Dan Gilbert, the booing of the Cleveland fans, the jerseys being burned—seeing all that was hard for them. My emotions were more mixed. It was easy to say, "OK, I don't want to deal with these people ever again." But then you think about the other side. What if I were a kid who looked up to an athlete, and that athlete made me want to do better in my own life, and then he left? How would I react? I've met with Dan, face-to-face, man-to-man. We've talked it out. Everybody makes mistakes. I've made mistakes as well. Who am I to hold a grudge?

I'm not promising a championship. I know how hard that is to deliver. We're not ready right now. No way. Of course, I want to win next year, but I'm realistic. It will be a long process, much longer than it was in 2010. My patience will get tested. I know that. I'm going into a situation with a young team and a new coach. I will be the old head. But I get a thrill out of bringing a group together and helping them reach a place they didn't know they could go. I see myself as a mentor now and I'm excited to lead some of these talented young guys. I think I can help Kyrie Irving become one of the best point guards in our league. I think I can help elevate Tristan Thompson and Dion Waiters. And I can't wait to reunite with Anderson Varejão, one of my favorite teammates.

But this is not about the roster or the organization. I feel my calling here goes above basketball. I have a responsibility to lead, in more ways than one, and I take that very seriously. My presence can make a difference in Miami, but I think it can mean more where I'm from. I want kids in Northeast Ohio, like the hundreds of Akron third-graders I sponsor through my foundation, to realize that there's no better place to grow up. Maybe some of them will come home after college and start a family or open a business. That would make me smile. Our community, which has struggled so much, needs all the talent it can get.

In Northeast Ohio, nothing is given. Everything is earned. You work for what you have.

I'm ready to accept the challenge. I'm coming home.

Ken Carman later provided his opinion on why LeBron chose to come back home:

It wasn't the Cavaliers or Dan Gilbert, it was his family. It is what he wants to build here, but it is hard to trust a guy who has so many options. When you are the most powerful figure in sports, it is hard to trust that man because he has so many people who are trying to offer him something better to try and take him away from you. I guarantee he will opt out of his contract early and people will freak out. I don't believe he will ever leave, but he will opt out of his contract. All the ESPN NBA beat reporters will fire it all up again and start the reports of him leaving because someone will make him an offer the way the Knicks made Michael Jordan an offer. You have to try and trust a person. To see that essay that LeBron wrote, it is just so bad business if he leaves again because he so desperately wants to leave. This is a guy who has 13 million followers on Twitter and he blocks people who don't like him. He wants to be liked and he hates being disliked. He hates being hated even here in Cleveland. He wants to have this connection with Northeast Ohio and this is what makes him special. LeBron James is a homebody and what he has done over the last four years, he has killed us with kindness. He has his logo everywhere, and people love him. He is just going to impose himself on us so that the people who hate him will start liking him all over again. He is the best player in the world, and we gravitate towards winners in this country and that is what makes America great. He is so good, and wins, and because he seems like such a nice person, people will love him again. I think this is about his friends and family and being able to come back home when it is all said and done and not have to answer a bunch of questions. He is smart, he knows his own mortality now. There is a part of him that thinks he may be walking around town and having to answer questions about why he left. People will always wonder what could have been while he was here in Cleveland. He needed to make this right because he is a guy who is in the community and who wants to loved. We get so serious about things in this world, about jobs and the economy, but morals are every bit as important. LeBron James can control morals, he can't bring back jobs but he can make people feel better. He can't guarantee a championship or anything but his absolute best effort. But if you have the best basketball player in the world and that incredible opportunity that many of us have never *had . . . there have been two generations of sports fans that haven't seen anything, and that is part of that morale boost that he brings. I think that it is a calling for him, that connection with the fans. We cross our fingers, but it is that connection that keeps him here for the duration of his career.*

Kenny Roda also gave his impressions on why LeBron chose to return to Cleveland and once again play for the Cavaliers:

The planets aligned, as there are a number of reasons why LeBron James came back to Cleveland. First and foremost, if the Cavaliers didn't have a strong roster there was no chance he would come back. So he looked at the roster and realized that the Cavaliers' roster as it is currently constructed with Kyrie Irving, Dion Waiters, and Andrew Wiggins, that was the first and most important reason he comes back home. His coming home was a huge factor, but he doesn't come home if the Cavaliers suck, and the roster has the potential to be very good with him in the middle of it. I think he looked at Miami's aging roster with its lack of depth and looked at the Cavaliers young roster before anything else and said this is the place that gives me the best chance to win. If not in the first season, then in the next several after that as he tries to extend his career and win multiple championships. The second factor was about coming home and coming back to Cleveland/Akron with redemption and unfinished business on his mind to help build his legacy. So the perfect storm is the roster combined with redemption and being able to come home. Plus it doesn't hurt that he can get a max contract eventually and become the highest-paid player on his team. It was the planets aligning, the perfect storm, and everything just pointed to him coming back.

The essay from LeBron was pure class and brought a tear to the eye of every person from Northeast Ohio who read it. It was real, it was honest, it was humble, and it was exactly what he needed to say to earn full forgiveness and redemption. Cleveland was ready to forgive him, and the approach he took made it 10 times easier. The Chosen One had come home! This proved how much he had matured and that going to Miami made him a man; it showed him how to lead, and he was returning to a better roster now than the one he left behind in 2010.

LeBron's homecoming was celebrated statewide. A rally was thrown for him in his hometown days after his decision. Season tickets were sold out 9 hours after he announced his return. Basketball fever in Cleveland reached an all-time high.

After LeBron signed with Cleveland, other pieces of the puzzle quickly began to fall into place. New head coach David Blatt, along with new general manager David Griffin, went right to work acquiring more talent for LeBron. They had re-signed their 2011 overall first-round draft pick Kyrie Irving—the Cavaliers' best player, two-time all-star, 2013 All-Star Game MVP, 2012 NBA Rookie of the Year, and 2013 NBA All-Star Weekend Three-Point Shootout winner—to a max contract extension just before the return of "King James." Now the Cavaliers had even more leverage to start using in deals to bring in even more talent to surround both players.

The Cavaliers had won the NBA draft lottery two years (2013 and 2014) in a row and had drafted Anthony Bennett after winning the 2013 NBA draft lottery out of the University of Nevada, Las Vegas. He had a slow rookie season in which he battled injury, but people still believed he could play. In 2014, the Cavaliers selected Andrew Wiggins out of the University of Kansas with their first draft pick. There was a lot of hype surrounding Wiggins, and many fans and the

LeBron James returned to Cleveland in 2014 and met with his fans for a rally in Akron.

Photo: kennyroda.com

media considered his potential limitless. Griffin now had three number-one picks on the Cavaliers' roster with which to play. He made it clear he wouldn't be trading Irving after they re-signed him, but he also never said he wouldn't deal the other two if the right proposal fell into his lap.

The Minnesota Timberwolves had one of the best players in the league with power forward Kevin Love on their roster. He was on the last year of his contract and had stated numerous times that he would not re-sign with Minnesota. The moment LeBron returned to Cleveland, talk heated up between both the Cavaliers and the Timberwolves about a possible deal with Love. The sticking point was if the Cavaliers would be willing to depart with Wiggins and Bennett for the chance at Love. It quickly became clear that Griffin was willing to do anything to keep LeBron happy and didn't waste any time trading away both Bennett and Wiggins to the Timberwolves in order to bring in one of the game's top five players. Griffin had recognized why LeBron left Cleveland the first time and was determined to never let it happen again. It is speculated that this move will keep LeBron happy for many years to come.

The Cavaliers now have their very own version of a "Big Three" in Love, Irving, and LeBron. Despite LeBron putting Cavaliers fans through four years of hell after he left, like the saying goes, sometimes it's hell getting to Heaven. The glory days are here once more, and the Cleveland Cavaliers are once again the talk of the sports world. It is now time for Act Two of the greatest show Cleveland and the entire sports world have ever seen. The road to redemption begins today!

Epilogue

In the spring of 2003, Cavaliers fans were at an all-time low. Their beloved team had just wrapped up another 17-win season and for the fifth straight year the Cavaliers had missed the playoffs. This was something that never seemed possible during the team's glory years when Mark Price, Larry Nance, Brad Daugherty, and Craig Ehlo routinely made trips deep into the playoffs only to lose to the greatest player of all time: Michael Jordan.

If only the Cavaliers could somehow obtain a player who was destined to be the next "greatest ever," perhaps their luck could finally change for the better. Sure, there was this kid named LeBron James out there, a local talent who was setting the world on fire while still playing in high school. He was called the Chosen One, signifying that whatever team was lucky enough to draft him would instantly change its destiny. But this couldn't possibly happen to the Cavaliers, could it? It almost seemed too good to be true when a Hollywood script–like turn of events unfolded, awarding the lowly Cavaliers the number-one pick in the upcoming draft—a near-miracle had occurred.

Cavaliers fans slowly started to believe that the winds of change were finally blowing and watched as this young prince grew into a King on the court. LeBron scored 25 points in his first night in the NBA and never looked back. Despite a lack of talent around him, LeBron continued to impress and even win the 2004 NBA Rookie of the Year Award. Everything seemed to be going well when the team's second best player, Carlos Boozer, lied to ownership, became a free agent, and skipped town. LeBron remained unfazed and continued improving in his second season. As he got better, so did the team, missing the playoffs by only one game and just a heartbeat away from taking the next step.

The very next spring, LeBron led the Cavaliers back to the playoffs for the first time in eight years as he earned a triple-double in his very first playoff game. He also made two game-winning shots in that same series—his first in the playoffs. Suddenly Cleveland fans were spoiled with what seemed like an embarrassment of riches as they watched LeBron perform on a nightly basis. For the first time in a long time, it was Cleveland winning games on the final play, the final shot, and, for once, not receiving the cruelest twists of fate.

As the game winners piled up the following season and the epic game five at The Palace of Auburn Hills in the 2007 Eastern Conference Finals went down, it seemed more and more likely that Cleveland fans would bear witness to the greatest story ever told. Even after the Cavaliers were swept in the finals that year, it was widely believed that it would only be a matter of time before the best player on the planet brought Cleveland right back to the finals—the next logical step!

What unfolded instead was a pain no Cleveland sports fan truly deserved: an early exit to Boston in 2008, the final loss being a gut-wrenching game-seven slugfest in Beantown. The next two years had Cleveland fans watch as LeBron became the MVP of the league—

a league in which the Cavaliers held the best record in twice—only to be knocked out of the NBA Finals early each year. And just when fans thought it couldn't get any worse, LeBron went on national television and told the world—before telling his home team—that he was leaving Cleveland for the beach.

Cavaliers fans watched LeBron for the next four years, rooting against him and the Miami Heat every time they took the court. It was LeBron who thrived off the hatred toward him with four straight trips to the NBA Finals, including two championship wins and two more regular season MVPs for LeBron.

With LeBron's two NBA Finals trophies and multiple MVP awards (not to mention sunny beaches and no state income tax in Florida), no one thought he would possibly come back to a team that was still struggling four years after his departure. But LeBron wasn't just coming back to a team, he was coming back to a city he loved with a dream that was never finished—LeBron was coming home. In an essay that brought tears to the eyes of those who read it, LeBron explained that he had to learn how to win elsewhere in order to come back home and be good enough to teach his new Cavalier teammates.

Only time will tell if it was all worth it in the end. Will the pain of loss be replaced with a renewed faith and lead to a championship reward for Cleveland sports fans? Or will the Cavaliers end up right back where they started?

Appendix 1:

LeBron's 10 Greatest Games of All Time

LeBron James has played in 852 regular-season games as of this writing. He has also played in 10 All-Star games and 158 playoff games, and he's been part of three medal-winning Olympic Teams. What follows is a summary of his 10 best games. Picking them was no easy task, because when it comes to LeBron—a man who has been voted league MVP four times and Finals MVP twice—it would really be easier and more thorough to name his top *100* games. But one thing is for sure: No matter how his games are ranked, it's an honor and a privilege to watch the Chosen One play every time he laces up his sneakers and tosses the powder.

The Cleveland Cavaliers vs. The Sacramento Kings

IN SACRAMENTO AT THE ARCO CENTER

ll eyes were on the King as he suited up for his first real game as a professional basketball player. How would the 18-year-old handle the pressure of the world watching him on the big stage for the first time when the points mattered? At that time, Sacramento was one of the best teams in the league and was widely expected to become the next big team dynasty after the Los Angeles Lakers. Though this expectation would never come to pass for Sacramento—instead it was the Spurs that would build the next NBA legacy—going into the 2003 season, many still felt that Sacramento would be the team to beat with such superstars on their roster as Peja Stojaković, Vlade Divac, and Mike Bibby.

Cleveland's roster was filled with a bunch of no-names with the exception of LeBron James, center Žydrūnas Ilgauskas, and young power forward Carlos Boozer, whom many thought would follow along with LeBron for many years to come as a lethal one-two punch. It wouldn't be too much longer, however, until Boozer would show his true colors and play everyone in Cleveland for a fool. Nevertheless, the King was not intimated by the Sacramento Kings, and he took action right against the home team.

LeBron played 42 minutes, which was an awful lot for a kid who was used to shorter quarters and games. In fact, the 42 minutes LeBron played was the most of any player in a Cavaliers jersey that night. But the minutes played weren't the only thing LeBron led his team in that evening: He also led the Cavaliers in overall scoring with 25 points. This was a kid fresh out of high school coming into his first game and dropping 25 points on one of the then-best teams in the league. He wasn't done there, however, as he also dished out 9 assists, swiped 4 steals, and pulled down 6 rebounds. He was the best player on the floor, just as advertised. Those numbers are the kind fans typically see from a veteran all-star, not a teenager tasting the pro competition for the first time. LeBron was more than hype, and it was clear on his very first night that he would be placing the entire NBA on notice right from the start that he was for real.

The Cavaliers stayed close all night and played the Kings tough despite being severely overmatched in almost every area. This was an early sign that any team LeBron was going to be on would be competitive. The Kings eventually pulled away in the end and won 106–92. LeBron's teammates were little-to-no help with the exception of Carlos Boozer, who pulled down 11 rebounds and scored 14 points. LeBron's other starting teammates Ricky Davis and Darius Miles didn't last long following this game, as they were traded midseason when the coaching staff and ownership of the team realized these selfish players didn't mesh well with LeBron. With this first night scoring explosion, LeBron proved that he was ready to lead from day one!

The Cleveland Cavaliers vs.
The Portland Trailblazers

IN PORTLAND AT THE ROSE GARDEN

The Cavaliers traveled to Portland as part of a West Coast road trip in the dead of winter. They were a surprising 22–14 and turning heads in the Eastern Conference, as LeBron, who was only in his second season, had brought the Cavaliers to the verge of turning a major corner and becoming a real threat aimed at going far in the Eastern Conference playoffs. That night, LeBron recorded his first-ever triple-double live in Portland.

LeBron had been in the league for a season and half at this point but still had not achieved that elusive triple-double. He would eventually obtain plenty of them—36 and counting as of this writing—but that night was his first, as he scored 27 points in 44 minutes. He also captured 10 rebounds and 10 assists. What made this moment even more thrilling for LeBron was that his final assist that night came in the closing seconds, when he dished it out to a wide-open Ilgauskas, who was standing outside of the three-point arc and drained a trey as the clock proceeded to run. "Z" was not a three-point shooter, which only made this more special for LeBron. At just 20 years old, LeBron became the youngest player in NBA history to record a triple-double.

The Cavaliers hung on for the 107–101 victory and continued to impress and surprise in the Eastern Conference. Unfortunately, a late-season meltdown, combined with an ownership change, led to Paul Silas getting fired followed by the team collapsing and ultimately missing the playoffs. By the season's end, after all the turmoil and changes, LeBron's first triple-double would become a distant memory for some. But for the players, they remember their first, and for LeBron it was very special to share that with Ilgauskas, a man who would become his longest-standing teammate. As he has said many times throughout his career, it is not about his stats but about winning games—and that night LeBron achieved both!

NBA All-Star Game

IN HOUSTON AT THE TOYOTA CENTER

Playing in his second All-Star Game, LeBron became the youngest player in NBA history to win the MVP award, just one of many awards and records he would set with the title "Youngest Player in NBA History" wrapped around it. This was a true showcase for LeBron as he was teamed up with the greatest players on the planet and showed the sports world that he was on the fast track to becoming the *best* player in NBA history.

Starting alongside fellow NBA greats Allen Iverson, Dwayne Wade, Vince Carter, and Shaquille O'Neal, LeBron could have found it easy to get lost in the shuffle or overshadowed. Instead, he mounted an incredible fourth-quarter effort to help lead the Eastern Conference to a comeback from a deep 21-point hole, tie the game, and then go on to win 122–120 on the strength of his hot hand and killer instinct, personally finishing the game with 29 points. As the Eastern

Conference head coach Flip Saunders watched from the sidelines, he had to be thinking about how his Pistons would eventually try to stop the red-hot player he saw right before his eyes. This was another sign that LeBron had the ability to take over a game and that no lead against him was guaranteed. This was also a key sign that LeBron was able to rise up in big-pressure situations. In games like these, where many athletes would not have cared so much about a glorified exhibition game, LeBron took every game he played in seriously. When this game was over, the fans and media weren't talking about Kobe Bryant or the vaunted Detroit Pistons defense—they were talking about the King!

The Cleveland Cavaliers vs. The Washington Wizards

IN CLEVELAND AT THE QUICKEN LOANS ARENA

LeBron's first-ever playoff game was played at home in front of a raucous crowd in Cleveland. It had been eight long years since Cavaliers fans had had a taste of the playoffs, and they were ready to scream and yell for 48 minutes straight in support of their hometown team. Once again, all eyes were on LeBron, who was about to step into unfamiliar territory for the first time: Though he had won three state-championship titles in high school and was familiar with the tournament format, this was the pro level.

Cleveland's opponents that night were the formidable Washington Wizards, who sported one heck of a starting lineup anchored by their Big Three: Gilbert Arenas, Caron Butler, and Antawn Jamison. With rowdy fans whipping around white towels, it was time once again for LeBron to remind everyone that he was a big-time player who could rise above the rim in big-time moments.

LeBron showed that age was only a number that night and did not let his youth get in the way of another great performance. Scoring 32 points with 11 assists and 11 rebounds en route to a triple-double, the Chosen One's incredible effort was the driving force that led the Cavaliers to a 97–86 victory. LeBron was later quoted after the game saying, "It's a God-given talent. I don't know how the box score will end up at the end of the game, I just try to go out there and play my game." Further proof that LeBron was a team player focused on doing whatever he could to help the team win and not focus on his own statistics.

Some fans would say that despite the triple-double, LeBron would have his best game of the entire 2006 playoffs just two games later in Washington when the series was tied up at one game apiece. The Cavaliers trailed that entire game but used an incredible 14-point fourth-quarter effort from LeBron to come from behind and win 97—96. LeBron scored 41 total points and hit the game-winning shot with 5.7 seconds remaining. The triple-double in game one stands out because of its uniqueness, but one cannot ignore the game-five performance in a tied series back home at Cleveland that saw the game reach overtime and the drama reach overdrive. With the Wizards ahead with less than four seconds to go, it was LeBron doing what he does best—taking the game winning shot and draining in it over several Washington defenders. For LeBron it was the cherry on top of a beautiful 45-point sundae. All three big wins and showings from LeBron are more than worthy of a spot on this list.

The Cleveland Cavaliers vs. The Detroit Pistons

IN DETROIT AT THE PALACE OF AUBURN HILLS

It was game five of the 2007 NBA Eastern Conference Finals between the Cavaliers and the team that had knocked them out of the playoffs the year before: their hated rivals the Detroit Pistons. One of the early knocks on LeBron's career was that he couldn't get past Detroit, with the comparison that it wasn't until his hero Michael Jordan finally got past Detroit that he truly took the next official step to stardom.

The Cavaliers had played and lost to the Pistons in the previous year's playoffs that saw an epic seven-game slugfest between the two teams. Cleveland was a heavy underdog that season, but not so much this year, and many coaches and players around the league and those in the media were starting to express that Cleveland could actually have a chance in the series. Fred McLeod, a member of the television broadcasting team for the Cavaliers, shared what he felt about the Cavaliers' chances of getting past Detroit in the series in the following quote:

> *It really was a special year in which the brackets set up perfectly for the Cavaliers. I remember vividly when we clinched the division late in the season and Austin Carr crying because he was so happy. It was an emotional moment, and I had to look away because I felt myself becoming emotional as well. Donyell Marshall was red-hot in the series against New Jersey to get the Cavaliers to the Eastern Conference Finals, and it felt as though things were going their way. Mike Brown is such a hard-working coach, and I knew he would have them ready.*

The momentum and confidence was there for the Cavaliers, they just had to exorcise their demons. The series started off identical to the previous year's, with each team defending their home court and bringing the series back to Detroit tied at two games each. The Cavaliers trailed all night long until LeBron went into beast mode late in the fourth quarter and took over the game, series, and league all in one night. He scored the last 29 of 30 points for his team, including the final 25 points straight in one of the greatest single-game performances in sports history. He finished with 48 points, 9 rebounds, 2 steals, and 7 assists all in 50 minutes of play.

Cavaliers play-by-play man Fred McLeod revealed what it was like to watch and be so close to such an amazing game: "I was part of the pre- and postgame that night, so I was at The Palace watching it. I had witnessed so many great moments there over the years, but that night was truly special. It was a sign that LeBron had arrived and was the real deal. Also, I think it gave the Cavaliers the momentum they needed heading back to Cleveland to put them away in game six."

Mary Schmitt Boyer, who reported on the Cavaliers for *The Plain Dealer* for nearly 20 years, had this to stay about LeBron's gigantic night out, explaining why the Cavaliers were finally able to get over the hump and beat Detroit:

> *LeBron loaded that team on his back and was not going to be denied. The Eastern Conference was weaker that year, and the Cavaliers were able to take advantage of it. The team totally bought into Mike Brown's defensive philosophy. He did such a good job coaching younger players. The stars aligned for the team and they bought into the entire team philosophy. They were led by a guy on his way up, and they took care of things with a right-time/right-place mentality.*

The Cavaliers went on to close out the series two nights later, sending the proud franchise to the NBA Finals for the first time in its history. McLeod described the emotion of such a wonderful night and series:

> *It was an amazing and emotional night. Bobbie Gibson was on fire, and that's when the term "Shoot Bobbie Shoot" began. You had seen a team that worked so hard and deserved the win. It was awesome to look into the gateway plaza and see the fans going crazy with excitement. Cleveland is such a great sports town with loyal, hardworking fans that deserved a winner, and they finally had a team going to the NBA Finals. Cleveland has the best fans in sports, and they proved how passionate they were that night.*

One could successfully argue that this was the greatest night of LeBron's career: It was the first time he took a team and squarely placed them on his back to get a momentous win. It was also the first time the city of Cleveland was on the winning end of a classic sports moment in NBA history.

The Cleveland Cavaliers vs. The Orlando Magic

IN CLEVELAND AT THE QUICKEN LOANS ARENA

lready down 1–0 in the Eastern Conference Finals series against the underdog Orlando Magic, it was desperation time for the highly favored Cleveland Cavaliers who were once again losing in the closing seconds. The Cavaliers blew a huge lead in game one and allowed the Magic to steal the first game in the series. LeBron had scored 49 points in game one, and the brilliant effort was wasted in a bitter loss. The team was on the verge of allowing the exact same thing to happen again in game two if they didn't catch some lightning in a bottle—and quick.

LeBron was playing the best basketball of his career, but without any help from his teammates, it simply didn't matter. As Mike Brown drew up one last play to try to either tie the game or go for the win in the regulation, those in the crowd and everyone watching worldwide knew exactly where the inbound pass would be heading.

To the surprise of no one, LeBron caught the inbound pass as he stood 25 feet away from the basketball, turned, and put up a desperation three-point shot that went straight through the net without a hint of doubt. It was the most defining moment in his six-year career at that point. It also was another reminder as to why he was once again voted league MVP.

The shot heard round the world played over and over again on ESPN and every other sports-related station and news program for the next 24 hours. It was the biggest moment of LeBron's career and also the most exciting. Up to this point, Cleveland fans had been crying in their beers thinking the team would be down 2–0 in the series and that a postseason choke was in full effect. But with one shot, LeBron had given Cleveland hope once more. No longer were there critics saying he couldn't close games, so long to the haters who claimed he couldn't hit the big shot—LeBron not only hit one of the biggest shots of his career, but he also placed himself permanently on all future NBA-playoff highlight reels to come. LeBron finished the contest with 35 points, 6 rebounds, and 5 assists. Above all stats, he finished by draining the shot many fans—children and adults alike—would mimic in their own backyards for a long time to come.

The Cleveland Cavaliers vs. the Boston Celtics

IN BOSTON AT THE TD GARDEN

eBron was fresh off of winning his second straight NBA MVP award, and the Cavaliers were locked in a battle with their sworn rivals, the Boston Celtics, in the second round of the Eastern Conference playoffs. The Cavaliers and Celtics had split the first two games of the series, then moved on to the hostile TD Garden with rabid Boston fans ready to scream and root on their beloved Celtics.

LeBron showed quickly that he had other ideas and came out of the tunnel like a house on fire, completely dominating the first quarter. The Cavaliers crushed the Celtics in the first quarter and led 36–17. In the first quarter, LeBron scored 21 points on 10 shots with 5 free throw attempts. By halftime, he had scored 28 of his team's 65 total points, and the Celtics were clueless about how to stop him. By the time the game was over, LeBron finished with 38 points, and it

179

would have been a lot more than that had he not sat out for most of the final frame. It was one of his finest games as a Cleveland Cavalier, with the team winning 124–95 to take a 2–1 lead in the series. It would also be his last victory in his initial stint as a Cleveland Cavalier.

GAME 8:

JUNE 7, 2012

The Miami Heat vs. The Boston Celtics

IN BOSTON AT THE TD GARDEN

eBron's last big game with the Cavaliers came against the Boston Celtics. His first huge performance with his new team, the Miami Heat, would come against the exact same team in the exact same arena. With the Heat down in the Eastern Conference championship series 3–2 and the national media just waiting for the Heat to fold, LeBron came out with other ideas.

LeBron dominated from start to finish in a blowout win over the Celtics, taking control of the game from the opening tip and scoring 45 points while pulling down 15 rebounds, with 30 of his 45 points coming in the first half. LeBron knew that if he was going to achieve his first championship he would have to take control and win it—and that is exactly what he did!

GAME 9:

JUNE 21, 2012

The Miami Heat vs. The Oklahoma City Thunder

IN MIAMI AT THE AMERICAN AIRLINES ARENA

With the Heat up 3–1 in the NBA Finals against Kevin Durant and the Oklahoma City Thunder, LeBron was just one win away from finally achieving his first NBA championship. He was so close he could almost taste it, and nothing was going to stop him from holding up the championship trophy.

LeBron came out stronger than ever and never slowed down. The Heat led by 5 points after the first quarter and by 10 at the half. They didn't slow things down in the third quarter either, outscoring the Thunder 36–22 to take a commanding 24-point lead heading into the fourth. Despite a valiant attempt at a comeback in the final quarter, it was too little too late for the Thunder. LeBron became an NBA champion for the first time when the Heat won 121–106.

This epic victory finally allowed LeBron to put away the distraction of his decision to leave Cleveland and move past the demons that had been haunting him. He was able to take the monkey off of his back once and for all with an amazing game-five effort that saw him score 26 points, hand out 13 assists, and pull down 11 rebounds. His series was impressive enough to earn him NBA Finals MVP honors, averaging 28.6 points, 10.2 rebounds, and 7.4 assists in the finals. After the win that night of the series, fans stopped considering him as the greatest never to win a championship, the media stopped dwelling on his decision, and, for the first time in his pro career, LeBron was a champion!

The Miami Heat
VS.
The Cleveland Cavaliers

IN CLEVELAND AT THE QUICKEN LOANS ARENA

Drama was at an all-time high as the visiting Miami Heat entered a hostile but also emotionally split Cleveland crowd for the eighth time since LeBron left for South Beach. Rumors were already running rampant that LeBron would opt out of his contract at the end of the year and return to Cleveland. This left fans with a mix of emotions and created a bizarre atmosphere for the two teams. In a previous game at Quicken Loans with LeBron and the Heat, a young fan actually rushed the court with a shirt that begged LeBron to come back home.

It was no secret that most Cleveland fans hoped that this would be the last time they would have to bear this pain, as they prayed that LeBron would come home with most Cleveland fans actually cheering for him throughout the game against the Cavaliers. This was a major difference from his first trip home, when the entire crowd booed him loudly every time he touched the ball and chanted nasty names at him throughout the entire game.

Inspired by the sudden cheers he was hearing, LeBron exploded across the court all night long and brought his very best game against the Cavaliers that night. The Chosen One scored 43 points while pulling down 6 rebounds with 4 assists. He once again had to carry his team because his so-called cocaptain Dwayne Wade was sitting out for another one of his 29 games as he was allowed to rest due to injury that season. The Heat won 100–96, pushing LeBron's record to 15–1 against his former team.

Appendix 2:

LeBron James vs. the Greatest Players of All Time

Throughout sports history to the present day, sports fans continually debate over two great athletes in the same sport that never had the chance to face one another. In boxing, the age-old question was who would win a fight between Mike Tyson and Muhammad Ali? Who was the better home-run hitter, Babe Ruth or Hank Aaron? Who was the better golfer, Tiger Woods or Jack Nicklaus? It is a question sports fans love to debate because there seldom is a right or wrong answer.

Since LeBron James first put on his Cavaliers uniform as an 18-year-old rookie, comparisons with some of the all-time greats have been common in evaluating his game. While some fans consider LeBron's best asset his passing skills, à la Magic Johnson–style, others tout his ability to completely take over a game with his scoring, much like his idol Michael Jordan. Here, we pit LeBron against some of the greatest talents in the history of the NBA whom he never had the chance to play against. Because such an undertaking can be clouded by bias, the categories are divided by statistical breakdown and overall accomplishments, followed by predictions on who would win in a one-on-one contest.

Through 11 regular seasons and 842 games, LeBron James has compiled the following stats and accomplishments, broken down here by per-game average. (Stats were provided by Google and confirmed with **sports-reference.com.**)

Stats per game:

- Points   27.5
- Rebounds 7.2
- Assists   6.9
- Steals   1.9
- Blocks   0.8

Accomplishments:

- 9 trips to the playoffs with a 28-point-per-game average in the playoffs
- 2x NBA Champion (2012–13)
- 2x NBA Finals MVP (2012–13)
- 4x NBA Most Valuable Player (2009–2010, 2012–13)
- 10x NBA All-Star (2005–2014)
- 2x NBA All-Star Game MVP (2006, 2008)
- 8x All-NBA First Team (2006, 2008–2014)
- 2x All-NBA Second Team (2005, 2007)
- 5x NBA All-Defensive First Team (2009–2013)
- NBA All-Defensive Second Team (2014)
- NBA Rookie of the Year (2004)
- NBA All-Rookie First Team (2004)

- NBA Scoring Champion (2008)
- Cleveland Cavaliers All-Time Leading Scorer
- Associated Press Athlete of the Year (2013)
- USA Basketball Male Athlete of the Year (2012)
- *Sporting News* Athlete of the Year (2012)
- *Sports Illustrated* Sportsman of the Year (2012)

These are pretty impressive statistics, but how does LeBron stack up against some of the all-time best? Let's take a look!

Jerry West

Stats per game:

- Points   27
- Rebounds 5.8
- Assists   6.7

Accomplishments:

- NBA Champion (1972)
- NBA Finals MVP (1969)
- 14× NBA All-Star (1960–1974)
- NBA All-Star Game MVP (1972)
- 10× All-NBA First Team (1962–67, 1970–73)
- 2× All-NBA Second Team (1968, 1969)
- 4× NBA All-Defensive First Team (1970–73)
- NBA All-Defensive Second Team (1969)
- NBA Scoring Champion (1970)
- NBA Assists Leader (1972)

LeBron has the edge on this one—he has a slightly higher scoring average, and he's won one more NBA championship. Despite being a 14-time NBA All-Star, West was never an NBA Regular Season MVP—an award LeBron has won four times. West did have a great post-playing career as an NBA executive, winning the Executive of the Year award twice. We predict that LeBron will also become involved in team ownership and executive games once his playing career concludes.

Karl Malone

Stats per game:

- Points   25
- Rebounds 10.1
- Assists   3.6

Accomplishments:

- 2× NBA Most Valuable Player (1997, 1999)
- 14× NBA All-Star (1988–1998, 2000–02)
- 2× NBA All-Star Game MVP (1989, 1993)
- 11× All-NBA First Team (1989–1999)
- 2× All-NBA Second Team (1988, 2000)
- All-NBA Third Team (2001)
- 3× All-Defensive First Team (1997–99)
- All-Defensive Second Team (1988)
- NBA All-Rookie Team (1986)
- Utah Jazz All-Time Leading Scorer
- No. 32 Retired by the Utah Jazz
- NBA's 50th Anniversary All-Time Team

The bottom line here is that, despite Malone's scoring records, he can't escape the fact that he played almost twice as long as LeBron. Also, Malone had the greatest assist man of all time, John Stockton, to feed him the ball on a nightly basis, while LeBron has had to create most of his own shots throughout the years. Malone's most impressive stat is that he was 0–3 each time he went to the

NBA Finals, even with a dream team in 2004 with the Lakers. The edge once again goes to LeBron here, and it wouldn't be surprising if LeBron breaks Malone's all-time scoring record by the time he hangs up his sneakers for good.

Wilt Chamberlain

Stats per game:

- Points   30.1
- Rebounds 22.0
- Assists   4.4

Accomplishments:

- 2× NBA Champion (1967, 1972)
- NBA Finals MVP (1972)
- 4× NBA Most Valuable Player (1960, 1966–68)
- 13× NBA All-Star (1960–69, 1971–73)
- NBA All-Star Game MVP (1960)
- 7× All-NBA First Team (1960–62, 1964, 1966–68)
- 3× All-NBA Second Team (1963, 1965, 1972)
- 2× NBA All-Defensive First Team (1972–73)
- NBA Rookie of the Year (1960)
- 7× NBA Scoring Champion (1960–66)
- 11× NBA Rebounds Leader (1960–63, 1966–69, 1971–73)
- NBA Assists Leader (1968)
- NBA All-Time Rebounds Leader
- Philadelphia / San Francisco / Golden State Warriors All-Time Leading Scorer

E ven though both men own the same number of NBA Championship rings and NBA regular-season MVP awards, there's no escaping the fact that Chamberlain's incredible points-per-game and rebounds-per-game averages give him the nod. Faced with a 7-time scoring champion and 11-time rebounding champion, LeBron has his work cut out for him if he ever plans to catch Chamberlain.

Magic Johnson

Stats per game:

- Points   19.5
- Rebounds   7.2
- Assists   11.2

Accomplishments:

- 5× NBA Champion (1980, 1982, 1985, 1987–88)
- 3× NBA Finals MVP (1980, 1982, 1987)
- 3× NBA Most Valuable Player (1987, 1989–1990)
- 12× NBA All-Star (1980, 1982–1992)
- 2× NBA All-Star Game MVP (1990, 1992)
- 9× All-NBA First Team (1983–1991)
- All-NBA Second Team (1982)
- NBA All-Rookie First Team (1980)
- 4× NBA Assists Leader (1983–84, 1986–87)
- 2× NBA Steals Leader (1981–82

This is the classic dream matchup that leaves NBA enthusiasts salivating just thinking about it. These are two of the best offensive generators of all time, as both men can pass and shoot with ease. They both excel at making the players around them better, and if Magic hadn't retired early, who knows how many records he would have shattered along the way. The biggest edge Magic has over LeBron is NBA championships: Magic won five during his time compared with LeBron's two.

Kareem Abdul-Jabbar

Stats per game:

- Points   24.6
- Rebounds 11.2
- Blocks   2.5

Accomplishments:

- 6× NBA Champion (1971, 1980, 1982, 1985, 1987–1988)
- 2× NBA Finals MVP (1971, 1985)
- 6× NBA Most Valuable Player (1971, 1972, 1974, 1976, 1977, 1980)
- 19× NBA All-Star (1970–77, 1979–89)
- 10× All-NBA First Team (1971–74, 1976–77, 1980–81, 1984, 1986)
- 5× All-NBA Second Team (1970, 1978–79, 1983, 1985)
- 5× NBA All-Defensive First Team (1974–75, 1979–1981)
- 6× NBA All-Defensive Second Team (1970–71, 1976–78, 1984)
- NBA Rookie of the Year (1970)
- NBA All-Rookie Team (1970)
- 2× NBA Scoring Champion (1971–72)
- 4× NBA Blocks Leader (1975–76, 1979–1980)
- No. 33 Retired by the Milwaukee Bucks and the Los Angeles Lakers

A s a six-time NBA Champion, Abdul-Jabbar is one of the only men in history to have his jersey retired by two different teams: the Lakers and the Bucks. The 19-time All-Star and two-time NBA Finals MVP is truly one of the best players in the history of the game. But were Abdul-Jabbar to go one-on-one against the King, we're not sure he could handle covering LeBron's speed and strength. Despite the large difference in their number of NBA championship rings, if LeBron stays on his current course, we think he could attain better all-time career stats, despite the breadth and depth of Abdul-Jabbar's resume.

Bill Russell

The only stat of significance is this: Bill Russell is an 11-time NBA championship winner (1957, 1959–1966, 1968–69). At the rate that LeBron has won two championships over his first 11 years in the league, he would have to play nearly 50 more seasons to tie the record set by Russell. No need to continue with this argument: Russell > LeBron.

Oscar Robertson

Stats per game:

- Points   25.7
- Rebounds   7.5
- Assists   9.5

Accomplishments:

- NBA Champion (1971)
- NBA Most Valuable Player (1964)
- 12× NBA All-Star (1961–1972)
- 3× NBA All-Star Game MVP (1961, 1964, 1969)
- 9× All-NBA First Team (1961–69)
- 2× All-NBA Second Team (1970–71)
- NBA Rookie of the Year (1961)
- 6× NBA Assists Leader (1961–62, 1964–66, 1969)
- Sacramento Kings All-Time Leading Scorer
- No. 14 Retired by the Sacramento Kings
- No. 1 Retired by the Milwaukee Bucks
- NBA 35th Anniversary Team
- NBA 50th Anniversary Team

Robertson averaged nearly a triple-double for his entire career. He could shoot, pass, and rebound with the best of them. Six different times, he led the league in assists while not letting it affect his own ability to score. He was the 1964 NBA MVP for the regular season. Even with all those accolades, at 11 years in LeBron still has the better overall body of work, with four league MVPs combined with two Finals MVPs and two NBA championship rings. It would be a fantastic one-on-one matchup, but at the end of the day, the edge here rests squarely with LeBron.

Patrick Ewing

Stats per game:

- Points   21
- Rebounds   9.8
- Blocks   2.4

Accomplishments:

- 11× NBA All-Star (1986, 1988–1997)
- All-NBA First Team (1990)
- 6× All-NBA Second Team (1988–89, 1991–93, 1997)
- 3× NBA All-Defensive Second Team (1988–89, 1992)
- NBA Rookie of the Year (1986)
- NBA All-Rookie First Team (1986)
- New York Knicks All-Time Leading Scorer
- No. 33 Retired by the New York Knicks
- NBA's 50th Anniversary All-Time Team

Much like Charles Barkley and Karl Malone, Patrick Ewing came up during the same time period as Michael Jordan and could never crack the proverbial seal around the NBA championship trophy. Ewing did have a stellar career that saw him obtain the 1986 Rookie of the Year award and two losing trips to the NBA Finals. He was quoted once as saying, "I spend a lot of money because I make a lot of money." It was a controversial quote that cost him a lot of fans. This quote, combined with his lack of championships and never winning a league MVP award, makes this one a no-brainer: LeBron > Ewing.

Charles Barkley

Stats per game:

- Points   22.1
- Rebounds 11.7
- Assists   3.9

Accomplishments:

- NBA Most Valuable Player (1993)
- 11× NBA All-Star (1987–1997)
- NBA All-Star Game MVP (1991)
- 5× All-NBA First Team (1988–1991, 1993)
- 5× All-NBA Second Team (1986–87, 1992, 1994–1995)
- All-NBA Third Team (1996)
- NBA All-Rookie First Team (1985)
- NBA Rebounding Leader (1986–87)
- No. 34 Retired by the Philadelphia 76ers and the Phoenix Suns
- NBA's 50th Anniversary All-Time Team

No one can deny that the bad boy from Auburn University was one of the best power forwards of the 1980s and 1990s. He was a rebounding machine and an epic trash-talker. His departure from Philly to Phoenix was one of the first big bad-guy moments of NBA free agency that, in a way, set the tone for what LeBron would do nearly 20 years later. Barkley has also been very tough in his commentary of LeBron over the course his entire career. Although one could expect a few dirty fouls on a LeBron drive to the hoop, this is another easy win for LeBron, who'd be a clear favorite to topple Barkley in a one-on-one matchup—not to mention that LeBron has already had the better career and is still a long way from retirement.

Hakeem Olajuwon

Stats per game:

- Points   21.8
- Rebounds 11.1
- Blocks   3.1

Accomplishments:

- 2× NBA Champion (1994–95)
- 2× NBA Finals MVP (1994–95)
- NBA Most Valuable Player (1994)
- 12× NBA All-Star (1985–1990, 1992–97)
- 6× All-NBA First Team (1987–89, 1993–94, 1997)
- 3× All-NBA Second Team (1986, 1990, 1996)
- 3× All-NBA Third Team (1991, 1995, 1999)
- 2× NBA Defensive Player of the Year (1993–94)
- 5× All-Defensive First Team (1987–88, 1990, 1993–94)
- 4× All-Defensive Second Team (1985, 1991, 1996–97)
- NBA All-Rookie Team (1985)
- 2× NBA Rebounding Leader (1989–1990)
- 3× NBA Blocks Leader (1990–91, 1993)
- Houston Rockets All-Time Leading Scorer
- NBA All-Time Blocks Leader
- No. 34 Retired by the Houston Rockets
- NBA's 50th Anniversary All-Time Team

O lajuwon is widely considered by many NBA experts to be one of the greatest shooting big men of all time. He had the rare honor of being one of only two players drafted ahead of Michael Jordan in the 1984 Draft, Sam Bowie being the other. Olajuwon was in the league for 10 seasons before he won back-to-back NBA championships. After his second failure to win an NBA championship, LeBron took time to fly down to meet with Olajuwon to work on his game. It was a major concession for James, but one that did elevate his game to the next level. Both men have won a game seven in an NBA Finals.

Olajuwon won the Defensive Player of the Year award twice and is the all-time leading shot blocker in NBA history—for that stat alone he would win the battle of one-on-one against LeBron. It would be a fun matchup to watch, but the edge goes to Olajuwon in this case.

Elgin Baylor

Stats per game:

- Points   27.4
- Rebounds 13.5
- Assists   4.6

Accomplishments:

- 11× NBA All-Star (1959–1965, 1967–1970)
- NBA All-Star Game MVP (1959)
- 10× All-NBA First Team (1959–1965, 1967–69)
- NBA Rookie of the Year (1959)
- NBA 35th Anniversary Team
- NBA 50th Anniversary All-Time Team
- No. 22 Retired by the Los Angeles Lakers

Baylor was a staple in the Lakers lineup, both in Minnesota and Los Angeles, for nearly 20 years. Sadly, during that stretch, his team failed to ever win an NBA championship, coming up short a few times. Baylor's stingy defense would give LeBron fits, but at the end of the day, LeBron would be too strong and too quick for Baylor. This, combined with LeBron's two NBA championship rings and four NBA MVPs, gives the edge here to LeBron.

George Gervin

Stats per game:

- Points   25.1
- Rebounds   5.3
- Assists   2.6

Accomplishments:

- 9× NBA All-Star (1977–1985)
- NBA All-Star Game MVP (1980)
- 5× All-NBA First Team (1978–1982)
- 2× All-NBA Second Team (1977, 1983)
- 4× NBA Scoring Champion (1978–1980, 1982

This four-time NBA scoring champion never had issues lighting it up on the court. Gervin could match LeBron basket for basket. He was more than just a good scorer but also an excellent teammate, and the fans loved him. A matchup with LeBron would be fun to watch because both men are entertaining and bring in the dunks and high-flying scoring from all angles. In this matchup of careers, however, Gervin can't hold a candle to LeBron, who has the upper hand with NBA championship wins and league MVPs. It would be a great one-on-one game, but make no mistake about it—as far as careers go, LeBron leaves the Ice Man out in the cold!

Isiah Thomas

Stats per game:

- Points   19.2
- Assists   9.3
- Steals   1.9

Accomplishments:

- 2× NBA Champion (1989–1990)
- NBA Finals MVP (1990)
- 12× NBA All-Star (1982–93)
- 2× NBA All-Star Game MVP (1984, 1986)
- 3× All-NBA First Team (1984–86)
- 2× All-NBA Second Team (1983, 1987)
- NBA All-Rookie First Team (1982)
- J. Walter Kennedy Citizenship Award (1987)
- NBA Assists Leader (1985)
- Detroit Pistons All-Time Leading Scorer
- No. 11 Retired by the Detroit Pistons
- NBA's 50th Anniversary All-Time Team

This one-on-one showcase would be an all-time classic. Thomas was one of the most talented and competitive players of his generation, though he never received the respect that he deserved. Thomas was a two-time NBA Champion and also an NBA Finals MVP. His Pistons team put a stop to the dynasty of the 1980s Los Angeles Lakers. In a heads-up battle, though, Thomas would be unable to get around the smother defense and strength of LeBron, who would use his size and power to walk away with the win.

Larry Bird

Stats per game:

- Points   24.3
- Rebounds 10
- Assists   6.3

Accomplishments:

- 3× NBA Champion (1981, 1984, 1986)
- 2× NBA Finals MVP (1984, 1986)
- 3× NBA Most Valuable Player (1984–86)
- 12× NBA All-Star (1980–88, 1990–92)
- NBA All-Star Game MVP (1982)
- 9× All-NBA First Team (1980–88)
- All-NBA Second Team (1990)
- 3× NBA All-Defensive Second Team (1982–84)
- NBA Rookie of the Year (1980)
- NBA All-Rookie First Team (1980)
- 3× NBA 3-Point Shootout Champion (1986–88)
- AP Athlete of the Year (1986)
- No. 33 Retired by the Boston Celtics
- NBA's 50th Anniversary All-Time Team

Bird is one of the greatest players in the history of the NBA and would have no problem reminding LeBron of that all night long if the two ever played. Despite winning only three NBA championships, Bird is far superior to LeBron in almost every single way when it comes to his total body of work and overall skill level. If LeBron is ever able to take the next step in his career, he *may* reach Bird's level, but until then the edge in this one goes to number 33.

Michael Jordan

Stats per game:

- Points   30.1
- Rebounds   6.2
- Assists   5.3

Accomplishments:

- 6× NBA Champion (1991–93, 1996–98)
- 6× NBA Finals MVP (1991–93, 1996–98)
- 5× NBA Most Valuable Player (1988, 1991–92, 1996, 1998)
- 14× NBA All-Star (1985–1993, 1996–98, 2002–03)
- 3× NBA All-Star Game MVP (1988, 1996, 1998)
- 10× All-NBA First Team (1987–1993, 1996–98)
- All-NBA Second Team (1985)
- NBA Defensive Player of the Year (1988)
- 9× NBA All-Defensive First Team (1988–1993, 1996–98)
- NBA Rookie of the Year (1985)
- NBA All-Rookie First Team (1985)
- 10× NBA Scoring Champion (1987–1993, 1996–98)
- 3× NBA Steals Champion (1988, 1990, 1993)
- 2× NBA Slam Dunk Contest champion (1987–88)
- No. 23 Retired by the Chicago Bulls
- 3x AP Athlete of the Year (1991, 1992, 1993)
- 2x USA Basketball Male Athlete of the Year (1983–84)
- NBA's 50th Anniversary All-Time Team

Michael Jordan is quite simply the greatest athlete and player in the history of American sports. As good as LeBron is today, he still has a long way to go to even get into the conversation at Jordan's level.

References

Websites:

basketball-reference.com

clevelandcavaliers.com

nba.com

Media Personalities:

Ken Carman: Sports-talk-show host on 92.3 WKRK The Fan

Austin Carr: Cavaliers game-television announcer

Fred McLeod: Cavaliers TV play-by-play announcer

Jerry Mires: *The Sports Fix* radio host on 1420 WHK

Kenny Roda: Sports-talk-show host on 1480 WHBC

Mary Schmitt Boyer: Former Cavs beat reporter, *The Plain Dealer*

Joe Tait: Cavaliers radio announcer

FROM THE FORTHCOMING BOOK BY

VINCE McKEE

Cleveland's Finest: Sports Heroes from the Greatest Location in the Nation

No one can measure the heart of a champion. It is the one distinct quality that can make any challenger a champion. Cleveland has been a part of some of the greatest moments in sports history. The city produced a football dynasty in the 1940s and 1950, won two World Series and came within a few outs of winning a third, and the basketball franchise has risen from the ashes to produce a miracle—a Chosen One. Cleveland has had rookie sensations offering near perfection from the mound and has produced a soccer team that electrified the world of indoor soccer with multiple championships. The loyalty of Cleveland's fans is unfailing, as they have stuck by their teams in good times and in bad. The fighting spirit of Cleveland can never be denied—offering the finest in all of sports cities.

The Golden Years

There was a time in Cleveland sports when winning wasn't just hoped for, it was expected. There have been those in the sports media across the country who have made the mistake in recent years of mocking Cleveland's teams for not winning a world championship title in more than 49 years. What those broadcasters don't realize is that this city was built on winning and that its fans can and will survive anything.

Cleveland is a blue-collar city with hardworking people that support their hardworking teams. No matter the previous season's record, the loyal fan base in Cleveland is confident that the current season will be their season. Times have been tough for Cleveland sports teams, but it wasn't always that way. In fact, from the late 1940s through the early 1960s, Cleveland served as the marquee sports city on the planet.

Joe DeLuca, who grew up in Cleveland, has many stories about the winning years of the past. Things were much different then, and winning wasn't a gift but a birthright. Born in 1933, Joe had the incredible opportunity to watch the first-ever Cleveland Browns football game in person. Throughout the first 15 years of his life ,he witnessed multiple championship seasons, not only in football but in hockey and baseball as well.

The Cleveland Barons were a minor-league team in the American Hockey League who played their home games at the Cleveland Arena as members of the league from 1937 to 1973. The Barons won nine Calder Cups, which was the minor league equivalent of the NHL's Stanley Cup. As Joe once recalled, "The owner of the team, Al Sutphin, was beloved by fans for his aggressive nature in trying to build a winning team. The Barons were so dominant that most people around the country considered them good enough to be the NHL's seventh pro team. If it wasn't for a longstanding feud between

Sutphin and NHL president Clarence Campbell, the Barons may have been the seventh NHL team at one point."

Joe remembered having to take streetcars from West 105th Street to Euclid Avenue downtown to see games at the old Cleveland Arena. "The cars had the old stove heat in them and weren't very warm. We would try to sit as close as possible to the front to keep warm and not freeze." Braving the cold of the streetcar rides paid off when he arrived at the famous arena in search of another Cleveland Barons win. He fondly recalled the packed lobby area where fans lined up to buy tickets, not to mention the beer and soda vendors. Soldiers who were home from the war would wear their uniforms to the arena, bringing their girlfriends with them. It was a special occasion to go to the games, and everyone would wear hats, men and women alike.

The Cleveland Arena hosted great events such as the Ice Capades, circus performances, area high school basketball championship games, and even Knights of Columbus track meets. It was a long, narrow hockey rink, regulation-size, with stands that could comfortably seat 10,000 fans with another 1,000 fans standing. But with 90 percent of games selling out, it was always a packed house to watch the city's favorite maulers on ice. A general admission ticket to a hockey game cost $1.25, while a Grand Stand ticket cost $2.25. For those in the crowd who had the money to spend, a box seat sold at the hefty price of $3.25. Joe explained that most people at the time only made about $40 a week, so these prices were steep for the league's best team. The atmosphere of the crowd was very different, however, as "back then just about everyone who went to a game would smoke cigarettes. It was much more commonplace and the arena officials saw no harm in allowing the fans to smoke in their seats. A thick haze of smoke would fill the arena to the point that you could barely see the scoreboard. The fans who didn't smoke didn't mind because they just wanted to be there and root on their winning franchise. Fans back then were such diehards that it didn't matter where they sat or next to who because they just wanted to be there," Joe detailed.

Joe rooted for all players but held the Italian-American players closest to his heart. He explained that, being Italian, it was only natural for him to root for them, with his favorite player being Ab Demarco. Because of attending school during the day, most of the games Joe went to took place on Friday and Saturday nights with the occasional Sunday afternoon matinee. "People in this town loved hockey, and if it wasn't for Jim Hendy buying the team and sticking a knife in the Cleveland hockey fan's heart, it would still be around today," Joe said. In 1948, the Cleveland Barons won the Calder Cup again in a four-game sweep over the Buffalo Bison team. As thrilling as the victory was, it paled in comparison to the wild ride on which the 1948 Cleveland Indians were about to take Joe and the rest of Cleveland.

Joe's earliest memory of baseball came from sitting on his Italian immigrant grandfather's lap, listening to Jack Graney call games on the radio. His grandpa would have a cloth hanky present at all times. When the Indians were winning, he would keep the hanky nice and smooth, folded neatly on his lap. When things weren't going well, he would twist and bite on it in a sign of frustration and worry. Joe had three uncles who listened to the games with him—Prosper, Jimmy, and Rocco—who were New York Yankee fans because of Joe DiMaggio. It was important to Joe that he grow up as an Indians fan and make his grandfather proud, despite his uncles' love for the dreaded Yankees. Joe was such a devoted fan of the Cleveland Indians that he sneaked into League Park on off days and ran around the bases. It wasn't until then-groundskeeper Emil Bossard caught him and kicked him out that his fun ended.

In 1920, the Cleveland Indians won the World Series in seven games over the Brooklyn Dodgers. The series was unique in that it was actually a best-of-nine series. The amazing game five of the series contained the first World Series triple play, a grand slam, and a home run hit by a pitcher. Years later, the team's owner, Bill Veeck, moved the team from League Park to Municipal Stadium. Joe's uncle Rocco had a weekend job delivering soda pop to the Municipal Stadium. It was on these trips that young Joe tagged along just to run out of the truck at each stop and catch a glimpse of the inside of the ballpark. Memories like these only increased his passion for the team and strengthened his support. Then along came the famed 1948 season.

—

Richfield

Richfield Coliseum was built in the early 1970s and first opened to the public in 1974 as home to the NBA's Cleveland Cavaliers, the WHA's Cleveland Crusaders, the NHL's Cleveland Barons, and, in later years, the AFL's Cleveland Thunderbolts, as well as indoor soccer teams the Cleveland Force and the Cleveland Crunch. The Coliseum hosted major sporting events, such as the 1981 NBA All-Star Game, and showcased several professional-wrestling events seen worldwide on pay-per-view. It also served as a venue for concerts with big names from Frank Sinatra and Stevie Wonder to U2 and Bruce Springsteen. Hall of Fame basketball star Larry Bird even mentioned that Richfield Coliseum was his favorite place to play on the road.

The building, located in the middle of a large area of farmland, was 30 minutes south of downtown Cleveland and stuck out like a sore thumb. It was a massive structure that held more than 20,000 seats and was one of the first arenas to include luxury boxes. Joe Tait, legendary announcer for the Cavaliers, remembered his first impression of the Richfield Coliseum as "a beautiful building in comparison to the old Cleveland Arena—it was like going from the ghetto to the palace. The one question was if people would still show up because of the long distance many had to travel to get there. At the time that part of Summit County was surrounded by farms. It was in the middle of nowhere and there was a sheep ranch right next to the building. I thought it was an absolutely beautiful building."

The Cleveland Cavaliers had a new home; now they just needed to start winning. Cavaliers owner Nick Mileti built Richfield Coliseum for his recently formed basketball team. Until then, they had been playing at the Cleveland Arena but hadn't enjoyed much success. Since the team's 1970 opening season, the Cleveland Cavaliers hadn't had a single winning season. Shortly after the move to Richfield in 1974, however, the Cavaliers' record started to improve. The team won 40 games that year but fell just short of the playoffs. Joe recalled the 1974–1975 season positively: "Things were changing because we were starting to get better ballplayers. We had not yet won a lot of ballgames in the history of the team, so the upgrade in the talent of the roster was crucial. The fact that we came within one game was frustrating but also encouraging because it showed you how close they were to bigger and better things."

In the 1975–76 season, NBA Coach of the Year Bill Fitch led the Cavaliers to a record of 49–33 and a National Basketball League Central Division title. The team boasted a roster filled with talent, including Austin Carr, Bobby "Bingo" Smith, Jim Chones, Dick Snyder, and the newly acquired perennial all-star Nate Thurmond. Years had passed since Cleveland had won anything—1964 as the last time a Cleveland team had won a championship. The team's newfound success had fans across Northeastern Ohio excited about sports again. "After the horrible start to the season, head coach Bill Fitch made the trade for Nate Thurmond, which was the catalyst that turned that ball club around. Nate was a great player and also a tremendous leader. He came in and really galvanized the team to get them aimed in the right direction and then went on to win the division," detailed Joe.

Joe became the man lucky enough to call the action of this new miracle team. In his childhood, he had tried to play basketball but never fared too well, as he wasn't athletically inclined. He didn't have a television growing up, so any form of basketball he experienced came though the radio. In order to make money while attending the University of Missouri in Monmouth, Joe took a job as a janitor at a local radio station. The station offered him a chance to do two five-minute sports radio spots a day. In 1970, the newly formed Cleveland Cavaliers basketball team of the NBA hired Joe as the lead radio play-by-play man, a job he held until his retirement in 2011. It was an amazing career that resulted in his induction into the Broadcast Hall of Fame in 1992.

The Orange and Blue Era

The Gund brothers now owned Richfield Coliseum, so it seemed like a natural move for them to also purchase the venue's main revenue producer, the Cleveland Cavaliers. It didn't take long for the Gund brothers to shake things up by changing the team's colors from wine and gold to orange and blue. They also replaced the swordsman mascot to the word *Cavs* with the *V* as a net. Theses changes, although small, made a huge impact on the direction of the franchise for years to come. It was a new era in Cleveland basketball, one that would provide fans with hope once again.

The Gunds were new to the world of professional basketball, but it didn't take them long to place an NBA veteran in their front office to build the team: They chose Wayne Embry to assemble a team that could make a quick turnaround and once again make the Cavaliers a playoff contender. Born in Springfield, Ohio, in 1937, Embry attended and played basketball for Tecumseh High School and from there went on to play basketball at Miami University of Ohio. The St. Louis Hawks drafted him in 1958 before he was traded to the Cincinnati Royals. His pro career covered 11 years playing for the Boston Celtics and Milwaukee Bucks. After a lot of behind-the-scenes front-office work while playing in Milwaukee, Embry eventually became the first African American general manager of an NBA team after retirement as a player. The Milwaukee Bucks made history by having Embry as their GM for seven seasons. After his seven-year run in Milwaukee, Embry decided it was a time to take a break and stepped away from the game for a few years. In 1986, the Gund brothers brought Embry back to the Cleveland Cavaliers headquarters to begin building a dynasty.

June 17, 1986, would be a day that changed the course of history of Cleveland basketball for many years to come. It was on that day that the Cavaliers drafted Brad Daugherty, a center out of the University of North Carolina. Cleveland acquired the first pick, which Embry used on Daugherty, in a trade the day before that sent Roy Hinson to the Philadelphia 76ers. It was one of the smartest moves in Embry's career as general manager. Seven picks later, the Cavaliers selected Ron Harper out of Miami University of Ohio. Both players were highly touted college players. The Cavaliers then went on to select Johnny Newman, Kevin Henderson, Warren Martin, Ben Davis, Gilbert Wilburn, and Ralph Daulton in the draft as well. Embry was not done dealing yet though on that faithful day, as he would send a future 1989 second-round draft pick to the Dallas Mavericks in exchange for the draft rights of Mark Price, who was also a first-round pick coming out of the Georgia Institute of Technology. With the acquisition of Price, the Cavaliers now had three first-round talents on their roster.

Epilogue

began working on this book on December 6, 2012. My wife, Emily, had just told me hours earlier that she was pregnant with what would be our first child. It was a roller coaster of emotions that ultimately left me thrilled with the prospect of becoming a father. It also got me thinking about my 31 years on this earth and the fact that I still hadn't witnessed a major Cleveland sports championship. I've rooted for Cleveland teams my entire life, experiencing a similar roller-coaster ride of ups and downs. I knew that if my loyalty to my unborn child was as strong as my loyalty to my Cleveland teams, then parenting would be every bit as fun and challenging. It also made me realize that the story of the Cleveland sports fan—and the memories we share—is one that needs to be told. This is that story.

Index

About the Author

VINCE McKEE is a growing force in the world of sports literature. His first four books, *Hero, Cleveland's Finest, Jacobs Field,* and *The Cleveland Cavaliers: A History of the Wine and Gold,* all helped build his credibility as a top-notch chronicler of the impact of Ohio sports. He currently travels the country meeting with the public to spread the message of *Hero.* Vince is an avid Cleveland sports fan who enjoys spending time with his wife, Emily, and their daughter, Maggie. He is always willing to speak with his fans and critics and can be contacted by e-mail (**coachvin14@yahoo.com**) or followed on Twitter (**@vincetheauthor**).